AMERICA

IN THE

LATTER DAYS

BRUCE W. ASSAF

Third Printing 2013
Printed in the United States of America

ISBN: 978-1-4675-6910-1

BLOW THE TRUMPET INTERNATIONAL
A Sound Publication

CONTENTS

PREFACE

There is much confusion, many questions and heated debates on the relevancy of scripture and how it pertains in probing God's role in the affairs of the nations. In this particular case, what is God's role when we thoughtfully consider the moral and spiritual climate of America, a nation in distress?

In carefully pondering and considering the history of nations aligning themselves with scripture, both prophetic and otherwise, and the carnage of past nations, there becomes a frightful reality concerning the future of America.

Winston Churchill was quoted as saying, "We cannot understand the future unless we can understand the past." And, sadly to say, history has always revealed that it repeats itself. It is obvious, and quite alarming given the state of national and world affairs, the sobering thought to consider the future of America. If we have not learned from past history, then we are condemned to repeat it.

America is a great nation in great distress. Given the light and grace God has shed upon America, it is more accountable. God raises up nations, and puts them down. God judges nations based on the amount of light and opportunity they are given. Like Israel of old, their judgment was more severe than the nations that surrounded her. God cannot and will not endlessly tolerate His laws and statues being ignored, flaunted and rejected.

Sooner or later, the nation who forgets God weakens and eventually perishes in the process of their rebellion. History has declared this already important fact. If we then declare God is on our side, and *In God We Trust*, we must realize as He is our greatest hope, He is also our greatest threat.

The Bible is full of "hard-sayings", many because we don't understand them, or we don't like what they tell us. We ignore what makes us uncomfortable. God's Word is a double-edge sword. The book of Isaiah, and scripture throughout the Bible, as you will read, reveals God's warning and judgment that is clearly cohesive to America and the nations of the world.

"Within sixty-five years Ephraim will be broken, so that it will not be a people...*if you will not believe, surely you will not be established*" (Isaiah 7-9).

America was established with those who believed God. Now we are seeing America's great apostasy. How much longer can America be the established nation and world superpower it has been?

Those nations, any nation, who forsakes the Living God, those *who will not believe*, cannot expect the foundations to remain as they were. There are dire consequences. The nation and kingdom that will not serve *(believe God)* will utterly perish!

> *"Your own wickedness will correct you,*
> *And your backslidings will rebuke you.*
> *Know therefore and see that it is an evil and bitter thing*
> *That you have forsaken the Lord your God,*
> *And the fear of Me is not in you,"*
> *Says the Lord God of hosts (Jeremiah 2:19).*

Bruce W. Assaf
April 11, 2011

AMERICA: THE WAKE-UP CALL

It was the attack on Pearl Harbor by the Japanese that brought America into World War II. Up until September 11, 2001, it was the greatest surprise attack on American soil. Ironically, the very port of New York where Lady Liberty welcomed those looking for a new life was the ground that began a new age and a new war against the foundations of a culture and country founded on biblical principles, a nation who declared openly to the world 'In God We Trust,' a nation who knew deep within that God's grace and light was shed upon her. Then came America's wake-up call.

September 11, 2001, was in fact America's new Pearl Harbor. The events of that horrific and historic day have caused many heated debates among Christians as to whether 9/11 was a judgment of Almighty God on America. One thing is for certain, the Lord's protective hand over America was temporarily removed that fateful day. Listen to what the book of Lamentations has to say: "The Lord has withdrawn His protection as the enemy attacks…" (Lamentations 2:30).

There are a few alarming scriptures that reveal to the Church, and our nation, the startling and frightful reality

1

that brings any debate to a deafening silence. It was evident God did remove His hand of protection. When 19 Islamic extremists, who were nearly caught, carried out their diabolical plan, America, a world superpower of 300 million was brought to a crippling standstill, in a state of chaos and fear.

When Ann Graham Lotz was interviewed on national television the day after September 11, 2001, interviewer Jane Clayson's first question directed to Anne Graham-Lotz was: "If God is good, how could God let this happen?"

Lotz replied, "God is angry when He sees something like this. And, I would say that for several years now, Americans, in a sense, have shaken their fists at God and said, "God, we want You out of our schools. We want You out of our government. We want You out of our business. We want You out of our marketplace. And God, who is a gentleman, has quietly backed out of our national and political life, removing His hand of blessings and protection."

In America today God is consistently banished from economics, science, history, education and government. We are told by today's liberals that the role of religion is to bless the soul, but it cannot interfere with our lifestyle and/ or public policy. Our nation has disdained and put aside God's judgments and statues. Yet, we cannot deny the relevancy of God's word in the affairs of history and nations, nor can we explain them away.

America has offended a holy God. The Supreme Court has made decisions that have insulted the Almighty. We are seeing His judgments as a result of our willful rejection of

God in American society. But, you say, this is America, "In God We Trust."A look at history reveals that patriotism can often replace the Gospel and the chief expression of Christian commitment. Patriotism has no power to save and does not invoke the blessings and protection of God without being in alignment to obeying His righteous statues and judgments.

We read in the book of Leviticus the alarming and sobering righteous judgments of a holy God: "...and if you despise My statues, or if your soul abhors My judgments...

1. I also will even appoint terror over you (vs. 17),

2. I will set my face against you and you shall be defeated by your enemies,

3. Those that hate you shall reign over you and you shall flee when no one pursues you,

4. And finally, in verse 19 we read, "I will break the pride of your power..." (Leviticus 26:15-19).

5. In the book of Isaiah we find the truth of scripture: "I am the Lord, and there is no other; I form the light and create darkness, I make peace and create calamity; I, the Lord, do all these things." (Isaiah 45:6, 7).

Another look at scripture can easily identify how God's Word speaks of His righteous judgment and the relevancy to the horrific happenings on September 11, 2001. "Therefore hear this now, you who are given to pleasures, Who dwell securely, Who say in your heart, I am, and there is no one else beside me; I shall not sit as a widow, Nor shall I know the loss of children; But these two things shall come to you in a moment, in one day; The loss of women and widowhood, They shall come upon you in their fullness because of the *multitude* of your *sorceries*, For the *great abundance* of your *enchantments*."

Verse 11 makes the suddenness of such judgment when Isaiah speaks, "Therefore evil shall come upon you; You shall not know from where it arises, And trouble shall fall upon you; You shall not be able to put it off. And desolation shall come upon you suddenly, Which you shall not know." (Isaiah 47:8-11).

There is always some point in time where the rebellious heart and nation crosses a line that eventually breaks through the limits of God's patience.

It is more than just the removal of God's hand; it is the unmistakable evidence of a holy God allowing sinful men to work their evil deeds making them instruments of His righteous judgment.

God has always used ruthless foreign powers and enemies to bring His righteous judgment on those, like ancient Israel, who have known and are acquainted with His laws. What motivated God to commission an evil nation to judge His people Israel? We read from the book of Isaiah:

"Woe to Assyria, the rod of My anger and the staff in whose hand is My indignation. Will send him against an ungodly nation, and against the people of My wrath I will give him charge, to seize the spoil, to take the prey, and to tread them down like the mire of the streets" (Isaiah 10:5-6).

Even as we see America departing from God, it is a nation founded on biblical principles, knowing and experiencing God with a great number of His remnant within. It was and continues to be a wake-up call to God's people and the nation in which they live. Just as Daniel was not exempt from the national calamity that befell his nation, whatever judgments God brings to America will affect even His most faithful people. As the Bible tells us that believers are not appointed unto wrath (1 Thessalonians 5:9), however, the fact remains that to varying degrees national judgments affect all who live within a certain region or in the same country.

BLINDNESS OF HEART

When freedom is demanded and then things go wrong, and disaster hits unrepentantly, the first accusation and complaint is against God in asking, "Why and how could you allow such a tragedy?" When God has given us moral choices along with the freedom to accept and live by what we know is right, that same freedom has with it eternal consequences.

If we do what we please, rejecting and ignoring God's laws; and yet, insist He has to protect us from the consequences, this too is deception, blindness, and arrogance on our part. We are to be very careful proclaiming, "In God We Trust", when our actions and attitudes prove otherwise. President Ronald Reagan was quoted as saying, "We do not need to be asking if God is on our side, but we need to ask ourselves are we on God's side." While God is our greatest hope, God is also our greatest threat.

After 9/11 defiance and blindness of heart were all too evident as America declared it would rebuild rather than seek God and repent: 'The bricks have fallen down, But we will rebuild with hewn stones; The sycamores are cut down, But we will replace them with cedars" (Isaiah 12 9:10)

America's need for God was short-lived. The pride to rebuild and the forsaking of God has blinded the eyes of America. Listen to what the prophet Jeremiah declared: "Thou hast stricken them, but they have not grieved; thou hast consumed them, but they have refused to receive correction: they have refused to return. Therefore I said, Surely these are poor; they are foolish: for they know not the way of the Lord, nor the judgment of their God" (Jeremiah 5:1-4). He is the God of our civil religion whom America has come to believe as a deity without sovereignty and a god without wrath. Nevertheless, the God of the Bible is the Sovereign God of the universe, and by no means does He acquit the guilty (Nahum 1:3).

It would appear that the God our nation pays allegiance to is not the God of the Bible. Nevertheless, the God of the Bible is the sovereign God of the universe.

September 11, 2001, had a twofold message to it. *First*, it showed a nation that has repeatedly provoked God taking His blessing and protection, along with His favor for granted; and, then flaunting those blessings in the face of the Almighty by calling *good* evil, and *evil* good, proclaiming itself invincible only to find out its protection was removed. A mighty nation as America, which boasts in its technology, power and military might, is simply nothing without the favor of the One who blessed and favored it. It must be remembered: "The nations are but a drop in the bucket, And are counted as the small dust on the scales." (Isaiah 40:15).

When 19 Islamic extremists could carry out a plan to cripple and bring a superpower of 300 million to sudden standstill of terror, it is evident that no nation is above the rebuke, reproach and the displeasure of a holy and Almighty God. Anyone, any nation who places their might above a God, who puts nations up and brings them down, cannot expect His protection and favor while in defiance of Him. (Psalm 75:7).

It must be understood that God does not owe America any kind of deliverance from her enemies. No other nation has turned away so much light in order to choose so much darkness. America has squandered countless opportunities with the light given her. We can only draw on God's mercy.

While over 3,000 precious lives were taken into eternity that fateful day of Tuesday, September 11, 2001, the words of Jesus reveal the sobering thought for all mankind: "Do you suppose that these Galatians (*Americans)* were worse sinners than all other Galatians because they suffered such things? "I tell you, no; but unless you repent you will all likewise perish" (Luke 13:2,3).

Our intelligence agencies and military might alone will not win the war on terrorism. We must understand that America is not any better or worse than the instruments of judgment God uses, it is whether or not we refuse our own opportunity to repent and turn to God.

Secondly, while His hand was removed, there was the mercy of God to expose an ideology of a political system within a religious framework which has as its determined goal the destruction of what they (radical Islam)

AMERICA IN THE LATTER DAYS

claim as 'the great Satan' or Christianity's child. Without divine intervention, God will only allow evil to go so far. The nation who boasts in her strength was spared even greater destruction. "God's mercy endures forever." Lamentations: (3:22, 23).

> The enemy attack on the most powerful and prosperous nation the earth has ever seen, was but a foretaste of God's righteous judgment, allowing the walls of His protection to come down.

Like Israel of old, God gave us a perfect example of their rebellion and the consequences of that rebellion. Israel displayed the goodness and severity of Almighty God, but Lamentations 1:8 reminds us; "Jerusalem has sinned gravely, Therefore she has become vile, All who honored her despise her because they have seen her naked-ness; Yes, she sighs and turns away."

In her uncleanness and rebellion was her downfall. "Her uncleanness is in her skirts; She did not consider her destiny; Therefore her collapse was awesome" (vs. 9). Will America's collapse be awesome?

As we read in Isaiah, the prophet gives a clear description: "Therefore thus says the Holy One of Israel: because you despise this word, And trust in oppression and perversity, And rely on them, Therefore this iniquity shall be to you like a breach ready to fall, A bulge in a high wall, Whose breaking comes suddenly, in an instant." (Isaiah 30:12).

CONSEQUENCES OF REBELLION

Our nation is given to pleasures and perversion with its moral corruption on television, magazines and pornography. With what Isaiah had pointed out in those given to *pleasure* and the multitude of your *sorceries*, it is safe to say the word given to Isaiah is relevant to modern day America. However, the pleasure craze of America will not last forever.

Those *sorceries* include epidemic drug use along with alcoholism, and the rampant and raging sexual immorality bringing with it the bitter and deadly consequences of transmitted sexual diseases. Yet, the Bible tells us whatever we sow individually, or as a nation, we will soon reap a whirlwind of those seeds, whether those seeds be sown in good ground or rebellious ground. God is not mocked as we reap what we have sown.

Facts attest to America's sowing seeds in rebellious ground. Rampant sexual immorality has always been the sin and signpost that God has turned a nation over to its own sin:

- The widespread acceptance of homosexuality in America promoted by the gay lobby and now endorsed by the President of the United States himself is no doubt the promotion of perversion.

- The option and right which includes the barbaric practice of partial birth abortion and funding of abortion; with 45-50 million unborn babies being murdered in the womb since the enactment of Roe vs. Wade in 1973.

- The divorce rate is now over 60% in our nation. It is almost, if not equal, in the Christian community. It is the world's highest divorce rate and twice what it was in 1960.

- America has the largest prison population. Incarceration of prisoners is seven times greater than most nations.

- In the 1940's over 60% of our youth had Bible-based morals. Now less than 4% do.

- Child abuse and molestation have reached epidemic proportions.

- There is widespread drug and alcohol use along with sex and violence in the entertainment industry.

- An estimated 5 million Americans have attempted suicide; while there are 750,000 attempts each year in the United States.

- 400,000 people in San Francisco attended a 2007 parade of sadomasochistic homosexuals that included open sex acts. The first signpost that God has turned a nation over to its own sin(s) is rampant and blatant sexual immorality.

- The internet explosion of American produced and distributed pornography is a $10-12 billion a year industry. Pornography has become the *norm* in America.

American television shows and movies constantly undermine the traditional family. The United States of America accounts for some 80 per cent of the world's pornography, freely available in many countries. Those foreign nations with religious beliefs, such as the Muslim world, are appalled at America's perversion and lucrative exports of violence and sex.

The violence and sexual immorality in America today has far surpassed that of the days of Noah and Sodom. There is a beckoning for all men to repent just prior to a greater judgment to fall. America is on the brink of an economic and social collapse. God's Spirit will not always strive with man.

The average age of the world's greatest civilizations from the beginning of history has been about two hundred years . History has shown the carnage of many great nations that had risen to great power and influence only to fall through corruption and a moral slide within. How long can a nation endure with crime and violence from within, especially when the laws of God had been once known, taught and revered. Sexual immorality has always been the first signpost of God handing a nation over to the consequences of sin. With a sexual revolution, and a militant homosexual agenda raging throughout the land, the President has taken upon himself to have the Supreme Court abolish the ban on same-sex marriage provoking God's righteous indignation.

How long can a nation survive and maintain a moral and spiritual compass and foundation when the floodgates of perversion have been unleashed by the highest office held in the land. How is it that the president could place his hand on God's holy word yet dictate the demands to promote perversion. This is an open attack that brazenly undermines that which is divine and holy. America beware!

God dispatched two angels to Sodom, as they were shocked by the utter degradation and wickedness of ungodly acts. It was a society that mocked family values. It was a time when the perversion of Sodom was so intense and extreme no one dared to stop it. It was so out of hand that the angels had to strike these lust-driven men with blindness. After being struck with no sight, they still groped for the door to pursue their raging lusts that inflamed them (Genesis 19:11).

Benjamin Harrison was the 23rd president of the United States of America. He said, *"If you take out of your statues, your constitution, your family life, all that is taken from the Sacred Book, what would there be left to bind society together?"*

Is the most powerful and most prosperous nation in history that has expelled God from almost every area of American life under His judgment? Has God's patience worn thin? Has the righteous indignation and judgment of God begun?

Sin is a disgrace to any nation (Proverbs 14:34). How much longer do you think God will allow us to thumb our noses at Him, as America rejects God and His statues and judgments. America is in a time where it refuses to blush at the most violent sins this nation has ever seen. How much longer will a holy God, in whose name we invoke, put up with all the wickedness in America, before He says "Enough!"

> When men lose their fear of God, they also loosen the reigns of their heart practicing evil inclinations without restraint.

We read in the book of Romans God's judgment being exercised. In fact, it would appear that God Himself has given those who desire their sinful and rebellious course over to their perverse lifestyle. With His mercy and goodness flaunted, the spiritual law of reaping and sowing casts the rebellious and defiant down into an immoral slide and spiral. The scripture makes known *"God gave them over"* as we see in Romans 1:24-28.

"For this reason God gave them up to uncleanness, in the lusts of their hearts, to dishonor their bodies among themselves. Who exchanged the truth of God for a lie, and worshipped and served the creature rather than the Creator, who is blessed forever" (Romans 1:24,25).

It is God's wrath that is revealed in giving people over to the ravaging consequences of their sin. Sin brings its own worse punishment. The result of sin and neglect of God's grace and offer of salvation guarantees to anyone painful results. God is never mocked. We reap what we have sown.

R.C. Sproul made these comments regarding rampant sexual immorality especially in regard to homosexuality. He says that God "isolates homosexual behavior as the supreme loss of human dignity…the nadir of human corruption and dishonor". He adds, "…the explosion of homosexuality in a culture is in a certain sense a reflection of a demeaning view of man in general and an expression of the wrath of God upon that society." Sproul, R.C. "Romans." Focus on the Bible. Scotland: Christian Focus Publications, 1994. 46-47.

Whenever a society or an individual spurns the moral and spiritual attributes of God, it will not be long before the wrath of God is revealed. God's wrath and righteous judgment can be visibly seen throughout our nation. The book of Isaiah makes clear mention as to the expression of that rebellion. "The look on their countenance witnesses against them, and they declare their sin as Sodom; They do not hide it. Woe to their soul! For they have brought evil upon themselves." (Isaiah 4:9).

America is a country above all countries of which it can be said, "They knew God." Today, the very mention of God in many public places brings with it scorn. God's

name is derided, profaned, in some cases prohibited...
"professing to be wise they became fools" (Romans 1:22).

In Romans 1:28 we find the devastation that result in both individuals and national leaders that no longer think it worthwhile to serve and acknowledge God for the well-being of their own lives and that of an entire nation. "And even as they did not like to retain God in their knowledge, God gave them over to a debased mind, to do those things that are not fitting." A debased mind is one that no longer thinks for the benefit of itself and others.

The cost factor of spurning God's laws have produced rampant and illicit immorality, social anarchy dominated by violence, injustice and greed that preys upon the innocent.

By denying any references to God and by removing the Ten Commandments from public places, the Supreme Court has insulted almighty God. God has blessed America like no other nation on earth - a nation with extraordinary benefits and economic blessings, not to mention religious and political freedom. The abandoning of God in our society has devastating consequences.

There is a manifest hatred of God, shown as persecution of believers in Christ in foreign countries is now becoming more evident in America. The breakdown of the family with children defying authority has become the norm rather than the exception. As those who once knew

God, their turning away has brought a swift judgment seeing God turning them over to their sin and rebellion.

As the prophet Jeremiah said so profoundly, "The human heart is desperately wicked, who can know it" (Jeremiah 17:9).

Daniel Webster was considered one of America's greatest orators (1782-1852). He also served as a U.S. congressman and senator as well as serving as secretary of state for three different presidents. Webster gave a speech before the Historical Society of New York on February 23, 1852:

> *"If we in our posterity shall be true to the Christian religion, if we and they shall live always in the fear of God, and shall respect His commandments, if we and they shall maintain just moral sentiments and such conscientious convictions of duty as shall control the heart and life, we may have the highest hopes of the future fortunes of our country…*

> *But if we and our posterity reject religious institutions and authority, violate the rules of eternal justice, trifle with the injunctions of morality, and recklessly destroy the political constitution which holds us together, no man can tell how sudden a catastrophe may overwhelm us."*

America, the same nation that had at one time been dedicated to spreading God's light to the world, a nation that has rang out liberty and freedom for all, has now fallen prey to the most devious and perverse ills. It has now filled the world with the obscene and the cancers of the pornographic. A tolerance for everything opposed to God and a growing tolerance toward immorality. "Woe be to them that call evil good, and good evil…" (Isaiah 5: 20). Scripture speaks well of the sudden catastrophe Daniel Webster warned of and what America can expect:

> *Because you despise this word,*
>
> *And trust in oppression and perversity,*
>
> *And rely on them, Therefore this iniquity shall be to you like a breach ready to fall, A bulge in a high wall, whose breaking comes suddenly, in an instant.*
>
> *And He shall break it like the breaking of the potters vessel, Which is broken in pieces: He shall not spare (Isaiah 30:12-14).*

THE REALITY PRAYER

When Pastor Joe Wright was asked to open a new session of the Kansas Senate in prayer the usual politically correct generalities whom everyone expected was instead a stirring and passionate prayer calling our nation to repentance. He said; 'Heavenly father, we come before you today to ask Your forgiveness and seek Your direction and guidance. We know Your Word says, 'Woe on those who call good evil,' but that's exactly what we have done. We have lost our spiritual equilibrium and inverted our values.

We confess that;

- We ridiculed the absolute truth of Your Word and called it pluralism.

- We have worshipped other gods and called it multiculturalism.

- We have endorsed perversion and called it an alternative lifestyle.

- We have exploited the poor and called it lottery.

- We have neglected the needy and called it self- preservation.

- We have rewarded laziness and called it welfare.

- We have killed our unborn and called it a choice.

- We have shot abortionists and called it justice.

- We have neglected to disciple our children and called it building self-esteem.

- We have coveted our neighbor's possessions and called it ambition.

- We have polluted the air with profanity and por-nography and called it freedom of expression.

- We have ridiculed the time-honored values of our forefathers and called it enlightenment.

Search us, O God, and know our hearts today; cleanse us from every sin and set us free. Guide and bless these men and women who have been sent here by the people of Kansas, and who have been ordained by You to govern this great state. Grant them the wisdom to rule, and may their decisions direct us to the center of Your will. I ask it in the name of Your Son, the living savior, Jesus Christ, Amen."

In an atmosphere charged with political correctness, like then prophet Daniel of old, this pastor refused to bow. With spiritual backbone, he stood before Almighty God as his prayer sent shock waves through the Kansas Senate. Provoking many who walked out and compelling others with their won "amen's". Afterwards, as the dust had set-tled, 5,000 unsolicited calls were made to the church. 90% were positive affirmations attesting to the fact that millions of Americans are angry at the moral decline of our nation and want their voices to be heard.

As it has been said, "all it takes for evil to prevail is for good men to do nothing." Billy Graham once said, 'It's not that people don't know what is right or wrong, they don't do what is right."

What we do with the blessings God has given to us as a nation is obvious. Remember, He has the power to remove all of His blessings, protection, wealth and resources. God does not merely bless people and nations. He curses them as well as a result of their rebellion and defiance.

One must remember that it is God who raises up a nation and puts it down. Inventing pretty names for sin and rebellion cannot blind the eyes of God nor reverse His judgment.

✕ God tells us from His Word: "See I am setting before you today a blessing and a curse - a blessing if you obey the commandments of the Lord your God, which I command you today, and the curse, if you do not obey the commandments of the Lord your God, but turn aside from the way that I am commanding you today, to go after other gods that you have not know" (Deuteronomy 11:26-28).

Obviously, God is already removing the blessings He has given to America. Why? He is doing it because America has rejected godly values. When any nation ignores the Almighty, and prefers the false gods of money, immorality and human secularism, God's righteous judgment will be a sure thing. He will not be mocked. He tells us; "Then I said to them, 'Each of you, throw away the abominations which are before his eyes, and do not defile yourselves with the idols of Egypt. I am the Lord your God' (Ezekiel 20:7).

America has given God lip service. The prayers of our nations leaders are prayers of wickedness, laced with propriety. They cover evil with pomp and circumstance, thinking all is well because they are in power, but they are not in power. Their legacy will not stand as one of honor, but of wickedness, debauchery and death to holiness.

The sins of America have been committed in the context of great light and great opportunity.

The words of Thomas Jefferson, although practicing his own version of the New Testament which removed the miracles and references to Jesus' divinity, did have enough knowledge of God to assert, *"I tremble when I think that God is just and His justice cannot sleep forever."*

America is now like the nation of ancient Israel as described by Jeremiah: "…Their houses are full of deceit: therefore they are become great, and waxen rich. They are waxen fat, they shine…Shall I not visit for these things? Saith the Lord: shall not My soul be avenged on such a nation as this? (Jeremiah 5:27-29).

The intensity of God's righteous judgment can only continue with wide spread devastation in an even greater way as our nation pushes the Almighty further away. The fate of America, and the terms of her demise, whether gradual or sudden, are in the making.

Abraham Lincoln made a statement that is more relevant today for America than at any other time in our nation's history. He said: *"We have grown in numbers, wealth and power as no other nation has ever grown. But we have forgotten God...we have become...too proud to pray to the God that made us."*

Yet, it is the mind-set of our nation, even within the church, God has to spare America. After all, He's called us to evangelize the world. It must be acknowledged however, God judged the wickedness of His own chosen people; He finally destroyed Nineveh after they had exhausted their time of repentance and turned back to their wickedness. He took down Rome. Would it not be unjust of God in judging these nations and yet spare America?

If God is holy and just, and not a respecter of persons, then He must say to America what He said to wicked Israel: "I will surely consume them", saith the Lord: there shall be no grapes on the vine, nor figs on the fig tree, and the leaf shall fade; and the things that I have given them shall pass away from them" (Jeremiah 8:13).

A DOWNWARD SPIRAL

The average age of the world's greatest civilizations from the beginning of history, has been about two hundred years. During that period of time, these nations always progressed through the following sequence:

- From bondage to spiritual faith;

- From spiritual faith to great courage;

- From courage to liberty;

- From liberty to abundance;

- From abundance to complacency;

- From complacency to apathy;

- From apathy to dependence; then

- From dependency back to bondage.

In his book, What About Heaven & Hell, author Douglas J. Rumford had this to say: "We must not mistake the comfort and support of love for a willingness to excuse careless liberties and license. Love welcomes and comforts all who respect it. But love does not tolerate disrespect and irresponsibility...love may not keep a record of wrongs, but it does discern the nature of those wrongs. If they arise from willful disregard and cavalier selfishness, love quickly steps back. Even what we call unconditional love has one essential condition: that each person in the relationship accepts an appropriate level of responsibility."

The book of Romans gives us the righteous judgment that is deserving of those who neither respect nor find it worthwhile to retain the knowledge of God. It demonstrates and teaches that both individuals and nations cannot escape God's moral and spiritual laws.

America needs to understand God is not a respecter of persons. History has shown the consequences of those nations that have rebelled and turned away from the Almighty… "the wicked shall be turned into hell and all the nations that forget God" (Psalm 7:11).

The great nation of America is flaunting God's grace to the point that not only is God's hand being removed, but He is active in bringing His righteous judgment to pass handing even greater segments of our nation over to their dishonorable passions.

America has been the cradle of freedom and democracy. It was rooted in more biblical principles than any other nation in history, with the exception of Israel where we derive our Judeo-Christian faith and foundations that have given us our legal and moral codes; as we abandon these foundations, in the end, the result will bring the eventual disintegration of an orderly society.

Those who laid America's foundations saw it as a covenant with God, as with ancient Israel. This would mean that America's rise and fall, as the founding fathers saw, would be dependent upon its relationship with God.

If America heeded God's covenant following His ways, it would become the most powerful, prosperous and blessed nation on earth. America did rise to heights that no other nation had ever known. If it departed from God and His covenant, it would lose the blessings and be replaced with curses. We now see America turning away from God, rebelling against His ways. From subtly departing and ruling God out, now in a more blatant and brazenly way than in its past history.

If justice rewards those who respect the order and natural knowledge of things, then justice demands a penalty for those who don't.

The consequences of rejecting God as the Rightful Ruler and the refusal of His moral code engrafted within each person, leads to a downward plunge and moral destruction, resulting in the death of a nation. The Bible tells us that God is long suffering, not willing that any should perish, but for all to come to repentance (II Peter 3:9)

In his 1994 book, When Nations Die, cultural commentator Jim Nelson Black documented and identified 10 crucial factors. It is the inevitable fallout of rejecting a faithful Creator in not retaining the knowledge of God.

It also has afflicted past civilizations and has led to their decline and fall. These are:

1. Increase in lawlessness.
2. Loss of economic discipline.
3. Rising bureaucracy.
4. Decline in education.
5. Weakening of cultural foundations.
6. Loss of respect for traditions.
7. Increase in materialism.
8. Rise in immorality.
9. Decay of religious belief.
10. Devaluing of human life.

Our forefathers knew the value of the Bible. They understood repentance and the act of rendering their hearts in humility before the Almighty. They also knew family values, the sanctity of motherhood and marriage. There was honor, along with love and morality.

With so many today professing they are Christian, and with the over abundance of churches throughout the nation, we can see even ministries, churches and ministers being idolized. Pulpits remain silent on moral issues that are rapidly destroying the heart of America. It would appear that we are witnessing a generation that really does not know the Lord and His ways. "When all that generation had been gathered to their fathers, another generation rose after them who did not know the Lord nor the work which He had done for Israel. (Judges 2:10-12).

MURDERING OF INNOCENTS

As America's president pushes ungodliness in promoting perversion and the killing of innocents, and funding of abortions internationally is without question a nation losing its moral conscience. What we tolerate today, we will embrace tomorrow. The result is a culture of death and broken lives.

The Bible warns us that God curses all who shed the blood of the just. God cursed Cain, the first one to shed innocent blood: "...the voice of thy brother's blood crieth unto me from the ground. And now art thou cursed from the earth, which has opened her mouth to receive they brother's blood from thy hand" (Genesis 4:10-11).We read from God's Word, God promises to "...(make) inquisition for blood...he rememberth them: he forgetteth not the cry of the humble" (Psalm 9:12).

Herod the Great, caused the babes of Bethlehem to be slain, hoping thereby to have destroyed Christ, he was plagued by God with an incurable disease, having his inward parts continually tormented. In his greedy desire to eat having nothing that would satisfy him, his inward bowels rotted. Herod grew made with pain until he died a miserable death. God has sworn in His word to judge and cut off every nation that condemns the blood of the innocent.

The sin of shedding innocent blood is a deep and grievous sin against God. The wrath of heaven will not be withheld, neither His vengeance as every slain innocent cries out to be avenged by a holy and just God. God will cast to the very depths the nations and individuals who murder innocents and the blood of the righteous.

The wrath of heaven will not be withheld as the slain of the innocent cry out to be avenged by a holy and just God.

The reason behind the destruction of Jerusalem was because of this very sin, according to the historian Josephus. He wrote that because Israel sinned against God by the killing of innocents, even in the temple, he said... "their sorrowful sighing's multiplied, and their weeping daily increased. It was the blood of the just and the innocents that turned Jerusalem into ashes."

With the rapid downward spiral of America, it is dangerously approaching the point reached by other great nations before they themselves collapsed and disappeared. As America in these latter days, a nation in distress, continues its downward spiral, it is evident God's judgment is being revealed.

With continual rebellion and sin against God a moral collapse from within beckons the deeper judgments of God in all facets of American life, even to the level of seeing greater judgment that the Book of Leviticus speaks of when a nation continues to despise and abhor the statues and judgments of God, "I will break the pride of their power." (Leviticus 26:19).

The domination of secular humanism which controls public education, our government and the media has undeniably eradicated God from a nation where our founding fathers planted deep roots of biblical principles. If America continues to abandon and blatantly violate God's moral laws, the United States of America will no longer know the leadership role among the nations of the world.

The blessings, protection and prosperity which God alone has brought to America are quickly being forfeited as a result of America's great apostasy.

God's Word clearly reveals how the Lord had supernaturally delivered ancient Israel out of Egyptian captivity. Her disobedience and rebellion against God had caused their hearts to become hardened and they were reaping the dire consequences of their sin. Their continual rebellion and sin against God had caused them to be defeated by their enemies.

Ancient Israel was not only taken captive by their enemies, they were cut off from God and became a reproach to His name (Isaiah 63:18, NIV).

Many enemies ravage America from within, greater enemies threaten her very existence from without. Is America under God's judgment? The destruction of the family and the loss of the Gospel is a judgment of God. It has been brought about by our compromise and many sins.

With the undermining of the American family and the push to go beyond the definition of traditional marriage with same-sex marriage, Ronald Reagan, the fortieth president of the United States of America (1981-1989) wrote the following concerning family values:

> *The family has always been the cornerstone of American society. Our families nurture, preserve, and pass on to each succeeding generation the values we share and cherish, values that are the foundation for our freedoms. In the family we learn our first lessons of God and man, love and discipline, rights and responsibilities, human dignity and human frailty.*

The disintegration of family values through the redefining of traditional marriage is the destruction and unraveling of American society and future generations. A blatant disregard and disrespect of the family is the nadir of human corruption and dishonor, along with the absolute rejection of the knowledge God engrafted into the very heart of creation. Whenever men lose God, they lose themselves, and their nation.

AMERICA'S SIN OF ARROGANCE

Many believe that God no longer judges nations for their sins. Modern day Christians have not only lost the fear of God in their lives, but no longer believe that God rebukes and disciplines His people. They characterize God by His love and grace, but negate the fact that the God of the New Testament is the same God of the Old Testament. To borrow a phrase from R.C. Sproul again, "We allow for God's providence as long as it is a blessing, but have no room for God's providence if that providence represents some kind of judgment."

Throughout the Word of God, we see evidence of God's dealing with nations. His promises of blessing and warnings of judgment are both alike...they are conditional. Through repentance, even at the last hour, God's righteous judgment may be averted. Through disobedience the blessings promised may be forfeited. The Book of Deuteronomy speaks very plainly:

"And it shall come to pass, if thou shalt hearken diligently unto the voice of the Lord thy God, to observe and to do all His commandments which I command thee this day, that the Lord thy God will set thee on high above all nations of the earth and all these blessings shall come on thee and overtake thee...but it shall come to pass if thou will not hearken unto the voice of thy God to observe to do all His commandments and His statutes which I command thee this day that all these curses shall come upon thee, and overtake thee: cursed shalt thou be in the city and cursed shalt thou be in the field. Cursed shall be thy basket and thy store..." (Deuteronomy: 11:26-28).

The Book of Deuteronomy reveals that obedience to God's laws results in that nation being "set on high above all nations of the earth" (Deuteronomy 28:1).

In verse 15, we clearly can see the adverse effects and consequences of disobedience. Verse 16 is a clear example of American cities that are no longer safe and secure. God's word says, "Cursed shall you be in the city." If America is to reap God's blessings, it must "turn from its wicked ways." (2 Chronicles 7:14).

History has shown that America was blessed when its behavior and laws were based on God's commandments.

When we study the shortest book of the Bible, the prophet Obadiah gave us a striking account of the proud and complacent nation of Edom. It is coherent and relevant to modern-day America. It would be evident that God placed within the book of Obadiah scripture that every believer needs to hear and identify with. Those verses are literally true and apply to the United States of America as it is today.

From past generations to our present day, those nations and America identify as modern day Edom. In light of America's greatness, she cannot remain the light of freedom and democracy to the world without the ongoing favor of Almighty God. He warns through His prophet Obadiah: "Behold, I will make you small among nations; The pride of your heart has deceived you, You who dwell in the clefts of the rock, Whose habitation is high; You say in your heart, Who will bring me down to the ground? Though you set your nest among the stars, From there I will bring you down" (Obadiah 1:2-4).

It must be understood first of all that ancient Edom was protected by an inaccessible mountain. It dismissed any possibility of a foreign power of invading her. It was therefore the mind-set of the Edomites to say in their hearts, "Who will bring me down to earth?" Edom had great pride in her strength and position which led to total trust in itself. Pride was also its downfall.

The people trusted their nation's ability without relying on God for His protection from all their enemies. Their arrogance blinded their eyes. With lack of fear of God and trusting in their self-sufficiency, Edom's pride led them further away from acknowledging God. This in turn would set Edom up for God's righteous judgment as they progressed further into their rebellion and sin. Indifference and indulgence leads to independence from God. "The pride of your heart has deceived you, you who dwell in the clefts of the rock, Whose habitation is on high (vs. 3)."

The sin of Edom was arrogance that over time provoked national judgment of the nation. In Hebrew the word *arrogance* means pride, presumption and a lack of fear of God. The results of such arrogance is self-exaltation and a flaunting defiance of Him which causes both individuals and nations to despise God's Word and reject His ways of living. We can see America as a modern day Edom. Edom became engrossed in the sin of arrogance before the Creator, God.

Arrogance causes a nation to despise God's word of truth and reject His ways of living; it results in self-exaltation and a flaunting defiance of Him.

Pride, defiance and arrogance reveal what the prophet Jeremiah spoke: "They have lied about the Lord, And said," it is not he, Neither will evil come upon us, Nor shall we see sword or famine. And the prophets become wind, For the word is not in them..."because you speak this word, Behold, I will make My words in your mouth fire, And this people wood, And it shall devour them" (Jeremiah 5:12-14).

America over the years has had one of the greatest militaries in the world. WWI and WWII made it the superpower bringing liberty and a safe haven for those looking to live in freedom. Because of its great national security and military might it is easy to understand the mind-set of America and can be compared to that of Edom's.

"The loftiness of our dwelling place" is a powerful metaphor to the exalted position of the United States of America, known to be high among the nations of the world. Yet, September 11, 2001, showed America, and the world, that it was not invincible despite its superpower status. It was seen on 9/11 a presumptuous nation being attacked and brought to a standstill by those lacking any natural strength to destroy our nation. Another look at the book of Isaiah reminds us of the presumption and pride. "And He will bring down their pride together with the trickery of their hands. The fortress of your high walls he will bring down, lie low, and bring to the ground, down to the dust." (Isaiah 25:11, 12).

Like any other nation or individual person, God has warned us from His unchanging Word: "And if you despise My statues, or if your soul abhors My judgments...I also will do this to you: I will even appoint terror over you... And after all this, if you so not obey Me, then I will punish you seven times more for your sins...I will break the pride of your power..." (Leviticus 26:15- 19).

God sent His prophet Jonah to Nineveh, bring- ing a warning of God's judgment that was about to fall. Although Jonah was reluctant, having no compassion for Israel's enemies, he declared the destruction of Nineveh was on its way and called for the people to repent. They did. When the great city of Nineveh, the enemies of God's people heeded the voice of the prophet Jonah, they were spared, proving again from scripture that God is no respecter of persons and is merciful not willing that any should perish.

If a pagan king could understand the importance and the need to repent, and understand the drastic measures that repentance required and follow through with it, how much more should the people of God and the nation who profess their Christianity fear God, humble themselves, pray and seek God's face and turn from their wicked ways (2 Chronicles 7:14).

FOUND WANTING

Jonah brought the mercy of God and spared Nineveh, a heathen city. Yet, 150 years later, the nation that turned from its sin was again found wanting. Like Edom, it too saw itself as indestructible and invincible. Yet, it too was brought to ruin, brought down by its pride and self-sufficiency, a nation that trusted in its power, might and position. Nineveh is another clear example of God's mercy and patience; but also, His righteous indignation and wrath upon a nation that was weighed in the balance and found wanting.

Nineveh had fortified herself that nothing could harm her. With walls 100 feet high and wide enough for four chariots abreast and a circumference of 80 miles with hundreds of towers, Nineveh sat in her complacency. Her great wealth and strength were not sufficient in saving her (Jonah 3:8-9).

✝ During the same time period the northern kingdom of Israel heard repeated warnings not only from Jonah, but a few others: Isaiah, Amos, Hosea and Micah, who were all calling for Israel's repentance. Ironically, the people who knew God's laws and statutes would not listen to God's warnings through His prophets, and refused to repent (Isaiah 7:9).

History stands as an awesome and sobering reminder of this fact. It has been said the inventions of civilization are powerless against heavens artillery. Nineveh is a type of all nations that turned their back on God. Scripture reveals Nineveh was overthrown because of her sin (Nahum 3:1-7).

Jeremiah 18 speaks of God repenting. Listen to what God spoke through His prophet: "And at what instant I shall speak concerning a nation, and concerning a kingdom, to build and to plant it; If it do evil in my sight, that it obey not My voice, *then I will repent of the good, wherewith I said I would benefit them.*" (Jeremiah 18:8- 10). God does not merely bless people and nations; He judges and brings them down as well. All God can do with a rebellious and defiant nation is to destroy it.

We can only look back to see God's dealing with Israel of old. He loved them, sent His prophets, and finally sent His Son. His dealings with Israel then, and again their rejection today, for the most part, will bring them into the painful suffering of "Jacobs Trouble" prophesied in the latter days. God is still God, and He must punish sin through His righteous judgment and justice on any nation who continues in their rebellion and willful disregard of His statutes and judgments.

"Stand in the ways and see, and ask for the old paths, where the good way is, And walk in it; Then you will find rest for your souls. But they said, 'We will not walk in it.'

Also I set watchman over you, saying, 'listen to the sound of the trumpet!' But they said, 'We will not listen'" (Jeremiah 6:16, 17).

Could it be that since 9/11 we have seen America falling further away from her only true Source of blessing and protection? Has the Lord punished the U.S. seven times more in what we are seeing in our nation as outlined in the Book of Leviticus: a diminishing dollar, trillions of dollars of national debt increasing daily, broken homes, increased drug abuse, hurricanes, tornadoes, droughts, floods, famines, murders with increased violence in our cities and neighborhoods, along with the war on terror in which America finds herself becoming exhausted in dealing with radical Islam worldwide (in Iraq, in Afghanistan, in Pakistan, in Egypt, in the Sudan, in Somalia, and beyond)?

September 11, 2001, has sadly enough become a distant memory to Americans. Since 9/11 radical Islam, along with the rapid growth of Islam, has as its determined goal dominance over western civilization. An ideology that raises its doctrine of triumphalism, dominance of one's creed, nation and religion, continues its expansion throughout the world. The Chairman of the Islamic-American Relations is not shy to voice "Islam is not in America to be equal with any other faith, but to become dominate." America now appeases Islam.

Again, as America turns from her only source of protection it has opened the doors for the powers of darkness to invade and infiltrate. Islam is more than just another religion; it is a political system with a beard of religion, totally opposed to and in rebellion against the God of the Bible from where America has derived its foundation, faith and culture.

God has openly declared in His word that repentance will always bring about restoration. In Leviticus 26, we read, "*But* if they confess their iniquity and the iniquity of their fathers, with their trespass which they trespassed against me…then I will remember my covenant with Jacob and also my covenant with Isaac, and also my covenant with Abraham will I remember, and I will remember the land…and I will not cast them away, neither will I abhor them to destroy them utterly, and to break my covenant with them: for I am the Lord their God." (Lev. 26:39).

Americas' enemies can be seen as God's instruments of His righteous judgment, especially in light of a nation being founded on Judeo-Christian principles and the light that has been given it. God has always used ruthless foreign powers to judge His people, those who have been given His laws and statues. Like Israel of old, because they enjoyed greater light and were more privileged, her judgment would be more severe. Israel had an outward piety mixed with idolatry.

Listen to what God's Word says: "But they rebelled and grieved his Holy Spirit; therefore he turned to be their enemy and himself fought against them." (Isaiah 63:10). God's own covenant people found they could not take His blessings for granted. Scripture makes it clear, "Judgment begins at the house of God" (I Peter 4:17).

The prophet Jeremiah gave fitting and alarming words how God stands ready to execute His righteous judgment and indignation. We have seen the downfall of nations throughout history, as God raises nations up and puts nations down.

Startling as it may seem, there are times when God is described as fighting against His own people.

"If that nation, against whom I have pronounced, turn from their evil, I will repent of the evil that I thought to do unto them. And at what instant I shall speak concerning a nation, and concerning a kingdom, to build and to plant it: If it do evil in my sight, that it obey not My voice, then I will repent of the good, wherewith I said I would benefit them." (Jeremiah 18:8-10).

AMERICA: A NATION OF IDOLS

Scripture tells us, "Their sorrows shall be multiplied who hasten after other gods" (Psalm 16:4). While we hear "God Bless America" and "In God We Trust", we are a nation that has many gods. America is one of the most idolatrous nations on the face of the earth: a nation of secular humanism, which in reality can be defined as intellectual idolatry. There is the pride of education, the pride of nation, the pride of family, the pride of material possessions, the pride of position...and the list goes on.

When all of our focus is on our achievements, who we are and what we have accomplished, giving no credit to the Giver, we have removed God from our hearts and lives, becoming lovers of ourselves, proud, boastful and unthankful (II Tim. 3:2).

We serve our gods while giving God mere lip service. The Scripture makes it plain: "Then the children of Israel did evil in the sight of the LORD...and they forsook the LORD God of their fathers, who had brought them out of the land of Egypt, and they followed other gods..." (Judges 2:10-12).

When we look at Ezekiel 32:39 we find "the people sacrificed to idols and on the same day they came into My sanctuary". If idolatry starts in the heart what defines idolatry? It is when an idol becomes a source for us in any area of our lives. An idol takes the very place of God in our lives.

Then there are the gods of flesh. In Greek mythology they were heroes. In America today they are movie stars and athletic stars amounting to national heroes. While school teachers are not paid enough to make a decent living, top athletes are paid millions. The love and greed for money is the god of mammon. Marriages and materialism are what millions sacrifice in place of their home and their health. We see the results. The Bible clearly gives us warning while encouraging us how valuable life truly is: What will it profit a man if he gains the whole world and loses his soul (Matthew 16:26).

An idol can serve as a source of comfort, provision, peace and even happiness. It lies within our heart. Idolatry is defined through Scripture as covetousness or a heart that seeks its own pleasure for its own gain.

Idolatry is not limited to material things. Idolatry originates in the heart. We find in the Old Testament in Jeremiah 3:6. Judah was quick in walking after other gods by committing idolatry on every hill and under every green tree. Then they would go into the temple of the Lord and stand before the Lord and worship (Jeremiah 7:1-11). Their hearts were far from the Lord.

Scripture again tells us, "They worshipped the LORD, but they served idols." They mistakenly thought this was okay, just like the people mentioned in Judges 21:25. "In those days...every man did that which was right in his own eyes."

Idolatry in America has blinded hearts. To remain alive we must recognize and serve the living God. Dead idols bring deadness of heart. "The idols of the nations are silver and gold, the work of men's hands. They have mouths, but they do not speak; Eyes they have, but they do not see; They have ears, but they do not hear; Nor is there any breath in their mouths. Those who make them are like them; So is everyone who trusts in them (Psalm 135:15- 18).

GREED OVER MORALS

Godly principles no longer have influence in a nation and government who declare "In God We Trust." Greed is one of the greatest forms of the decay and corruption of a nation. Money rules everything in America's political system and dictates everything in every sector of American society.

1. The collective net worth of all members of Congress increased by 25% between 2008 and 2010.

2. The collective net worth of all members of Congress is now slightly over $2 billion.

3. This happened during a time when the net worth of most America households was declining rapidly.

4. According to the Federal Reserve, the collective net worth of all American households decreased by 23% between 2007 and 2009. The greed America now embraces is a sure sign of idolatry and robbing God (Haggai 1:9-11).

The American dream appears to be turning into the American nightmare. The good majority of Americans in all aspects of American society have come to the conclusion morals do not count. They conclude, let the leaders do as they please, all we want is a thriving economy. Prosperity, and not God, is what really matters. The walls however appear to be crumbling.

As America has grown ever richer, God has been forgotten in the process. Yet as we see greed over morals, the American money-machine is weakening while the national debt soars to over $16 trillion dollars. The Bible tells us of the attitude now prevailing in America " …they overpass (overlook) the deeds of the wicked…yet they prosper…" (Jeremiah 5:28). However, it is God who controls the economies of the world and determines the destinies of nations. He commands, "Thou shalt remember the Lord thy God: for it is he that giveth thee power to create wealth…" (Deuteronomy 5:28).

America has not acknowledged God for the abundant blessings of prosperity. The nation has robbed God while forsaking Him. God in his word warned of proud and arrogant boasting that claimed their prosperity was a result of their own doing, ability and human skill:

"(If) thou shall say in thine heart, my power and the might of mine hand hath gotten me this wealth…it shall be, if thou do at all forget the Lord thy God…I testify against you this day that ye shall surely perish…as the nations which the Lord detstroyeth before your face, so shall ye perish…" (Deuteronomy 5:17-20). Like all other nations who refused to acknowledge the Lord, America will be humbled.

America amidst the greed and abandoning its moral compass is on a collision course as was the *S.S. Titanic* who said "Not even God can sink this ship!" This American mind-set is an abomination to the Almighty, and unless there is a national repentance America will continue to sink in the mire of her abominations.

Rather than the wicked crying out for help and wailing over their great losses, there continues to be heard only the sound of boasting and defiance saying "we will rebuild, we're America don't you know!" Listen to what the prophet had to say concerning this attitude of arrogance. He writes, "...the wind shall carry them all away; vanity shall take them..." (Isaiah 57:13).

What Isaiah was saying was all of your greed, pride and arrogance will all be swept away by the powerful winds of adversity. And as they cry, the prophet tells them "...let thy companies deliver thee..." God is the avenger of such proud boasting, greed and ungratefulness.

As commander of the Allied forces in Europe during World War II, and later president of the United States of America, Dwight D. Eisenhower, a man who knew much about the strength of men and women in perilous times said:

> *"The spirit of man is more important than mere physical strength, and the spiritual fiber of a nation than its wealth."*

President Eisenhower went on to say,

> *"The Bible is endorsed by the ages. Our civilization is built upon its words. In no other book is there such a collection of inspired wisdom, reality and hope."*

The spiritual and moral fiber of America has been replaced with greed and immorality. Franklin D. Roosevelt's 1939 State of the Union address understood the vital connection between religion and democracy, but the significance of the unseen foundations that made America once a great nation. He said:

> *"There comes a time in the affairs of men when they must prepare to defend, not their homes alone, but the tenets of faith and humanity on which their churches, their governments, and their very civilization was founded. The defense of religion, of, and of good faith is all the same fight. To save one we must now make up our minds to save all."*

Christians are responsible for the government they live under and get the kind of government they deserve. If the Christian votes for men who ignore God's requirements and are not God-fearing but decree laws that go against God's moral and spiritual requirements, against His everlasting covenant, we are not only in violation of God's requirements, we actually invite the judgment of God. As we condone their policies of abortion and sexual perversion, being in admiration of man regardless of their position of the highest office in the land, rather than the holiness and statues of God, we have joined in their transgressions. We have also been an agent for the destruction of our nation "calling evil good, and good evil" setting the destiny of America.

Any political agenda that promise change while disregarding God is but a great deception that brings with it false hope, and in the end a certain righteous and fearful judgment for all who have turned away from their only true Source. Scripture tells us it is an evil and bitter thing to forsake God (Isaiah 30:10-14).

THE SINS OF SODOM

The sin of Sodom was more than sexual perversion. It was a pleasure-crazed society in open defiance of a holy God. Sodom came under the judgment of God for many other reasons: "This was the iniquity of Sodom...pride, fullness of bread, and abundance of idleness...neither did she strengthen the hand of the poor and needy. And they were haughty and committed abomination before Me therefore I took them away as I saw fit..." (Ezekiel 16:49- 50).

Jerusalem and her sister cities were no different than America today. They were caught up in society's prosperity. They were trading, building, feasting and enjoying life to the fullest. They had "plenty of goods" and "fullness of bread" with the pride of life, with an abundance of free time and proud of their luxurious lifestyle. They were so caught up in the moment Ezekiel's warnings of impending judgment were lost in the hustle and bustle. They mocked the preaching of God's Word. Sound like America today?

However, God would set a date where He would cripple Israel's economy and lifestyle. Look what the word of God said regarding Sodom's (Israel's) demise:

It came to pass in the *ninth year* of his reign, in the *tenth month*, that Nebuchadnezzar king of Babylon came... against Jerusalem...and built forts against and round about (Jeremiah 52:4). "Suddenly, in a time of great prosperity, Israel was surrounded by Nebuchadnezzar and his mighty Chaldean army. It would be a sudden devastation overnight. The Israelites lifestyle was changed completely."

On September 11, 2001, America was changed in an hour. Could it be that is how precise God in His judgments can be? There is a time and hour already marked when greater devastation will move against the economy and our lifestyle. And, soberly said, there is nothing that can change the set time of God's righteous indignation against a nation that continues to make every effort to defy and banish the Almighty.

The prophet Ezekiel was describing a time of lewdness and abominations he saw in Israel that was beyond his comprehension. Ezekiel made it very clear that God would move in bringing judgment on the nation of ancient Israel at a precise time. America is more abominable than Sodom. It has become the most proudest, ungrateful society in history. America has gone far beyond the flash point at which God moved against Israel and Sodom. America can expect the same righteous judgment of a holy God. He is no respecter of persons.

"The nation that will not serve Him will perish." (Isaiah 60:12). It must be remembered Sodom had no Bible. America on the other hand is like no other nation given the great opportunities to hear and receive salvation.

"Return to Me; And if you will put away your abominations out of My sight, Then you shall not be moved. And you shall swear, 'The Lord lives,' In truth, in judgment, and in righteousness; The nations shall bless themselves in Him, And in Him they shall glory" (Jeremiah 4:1, 2).

"But this people have a defiant and rebellious heart; They have revolted and departed. They do not say in their heart, 'Let us now fear the Lord our God, Who gives rain, both the former and the latter in its season. He reserves for us the appointed weeks of the harvest.' Your iniquities have turned these *things* away. And your sins have withheld good from you" (Jeremiah 5:23,25).

Sin is a disgrace to any nation. America has flaunted it openly with government approval while voicing the slogan, "In God We Trust".

Arrogance, self-sufficiency, double-mindedness, a form of godliness, idolatry, greed and many other *evils* have blinded the hearts of our nation in its headlong rush to abandon God for secular humanism, the belief that all of our nation's ill's can be solved by human effort and wisdom. We have robbed God from His rightful place in American society.

God has already said, "I am bringing disaster on this people, the fruit of their schemes, because they have not listened to my words and rejected My law" (Jeremiah 6:19, NIV).

The fact is, God never changes; He will always move according to His eternal purposes. We can discern from the scriptures that God is dealing with America in the same way He's dealt with all the nations who have forsaken Him.

It was Jeremiah who took it upon himself to acknowledge and confess the sins of his people. His 'holy pleadings' to the Lord should be the heart of every concerned believer in America. "Although our sins testify against us, O Lord, do something for the sake of your name. For our backsliding is great; we have sinned against you" (Jeremiah 4:7, NIV).

He went on to plead with God's people, "If you will return, O Israel," says the Lord, 'return to Me; And if you will put away your abominations out of My sight, Then you shall not be moved. And you shall swear, 'The Lord lives, 'In truth, in judgment, and in righteousness; The nations shall bless themselves in Him, And in Him they shall glory." We too must plead our case, individually and corporately on the righteousness of Jesus Christ.

AMERICA AND PAST EMPIRES

As a present world super-power, America's status is being increasingly challenged. A nation in distress: can America still cling to a general preeminence or will it decline and fall? History reveals to us of great empires in the past such as Britain, Spain, Rome, Babylon and Egypt fell from their lone super-power status. In his book The Fate of Empires and the Search for Survival, Sir John Bagot Glubb (1897-1987) described a common pattern of some fallen empires that went through a cycle of changes as they began, expanded, matured, declined and finally collapsed.

Sir John Bagot Glubb learned that while empires were different they all had similar cultural changes as they experienced a life cycle of stages that could overlap. Here's what he described as he identified these successive ages:

1. The age of outburst (or pioneers)
2. The age of conquests.
3. The age of commerce.
4. The age of affluence.
5. The age of intellect.
6. The age of decadence.
7. The age of decline and collapse.

Military, economic, political and religious developments all have influenced an empire's people to act and believe differently over time. The great Prime Minister and historian Winston Churchill observed, *"The farther backward you can look, the farther forward you are likely to see."*

We need to be mindful of God's perspective in regard to America and the world: "Behold, the nations are but a drop in the bucket. And are counted as the small dust on the scales...All nations before Him are as nothing, And they are counted by Him less than nothing and worthless" (Isaiah 40:15,17).

The prophet Ezekiel voiced God's Word that relates to America and the famine we see throughout the land in various forms from the economy to pestilences in many forms: "Son of man, when a land sins against Me by persistent unfaithfulness, I will stretch out My hand against it..." (Ezekiel 14:13)

Dr. Martin Luther King Jr., the great civil rights leader of the twentieth century said, *"Our lives begin to end the day we become silent about things that matter."*

THE CHURCH IN AMERICA

Jesus talked of a victorious Church. He said, "I will build My church and the gates of Hell will not prevail against it." (Matt. 16:18). Are we now seeing the church Jesus spoke of here in America? It can be fair to say, "As goes the church so goes the nation." With America, for decades relying upon its military might and world super-power status, America's national security and its secular humanism have together cultivated the prideful assurance of its state of well-being that the Church has embraced. "Ephraim has mixed himself among the peoples; Ephraim is a cake unturned. Aliens have devoured his strength, But he does not know it." (Hosea 7:8,9)

Rather to stay in sound doctrine, the church has allowed the same attitude of secular humanism to creep into it. A powerful reminder of a loss of strength and influ-ence and the neglect of keeping Jesus Christ first and fore-most, has brought about a lukewarm attitude with spiritual pride. Human plans and agendas are no equal to the Lord building His house through the guidance of His Spirit. "Not by power, nor by might, but by My Spirit," says the Lord (Zephaniah 4:6).

"Woe to the rebellious children," says the Lord, "Who take counsel, but not of Me, And who devise plans, but not of My Spirit, That they may add sin to sin; Who walk to go down to Egypt, And have not asked for My advice, To strengthen themselves in the strength of Pharaoh, And to trust in the shadow of Egypt! Therefore the strength of Pharaoh shall be your shame, And the trust in the shadow of Egypt Shall be your humiliation." (Isaiah 60 30:1-3).

Both the nation and the church are dangerously departing from true trust in the Living God. The reality of what we are seeing today is exactly what the apostle Paul had already described... "Having a form of godliness, but denying the power thereof... " (2 Timothy 3:5).

While many perceive the church as a local assembly, a building with a cross, the true Church of Jesus Christ is not an organization but a living spiritual organism with people having an intimate, personal relationship with Christ.

Today, we find a group of people carrying out their religious activities in their buildings yet having no personal trust and commitment in Christ. They are people playing church and going through religious motions but have departed from sound doctrine, with an emotional and musical expression of faith showing great numbers, yet not bearing the fruit of Christianity. True Christianity, however, has everything to do with those who have placed their personal and individual trust in Christ.

The Bible describes that the church in the latter days, the final days of the Church Age, will be a *"religion"* where the power of God is denied. Most church people today think they are following the Bible and claiming Jesus Christ as their Lord and Savior, but whether knowing or unknowingly, many are embracing a corrupt mixture of Christian traditions with no power to save. Their beliefs bear no fruit. The condition of our nation clearly demonstrates where the heart of a Christian America is today (1 Timothy 4:1-3).

Often programs and activities have supplanted the intimacy of a relationship to the Living Christ and have negated God's power, presence and true authority. These distractions from our *"first love"*, keep the people of God without true fruit and authority in their lives. "In vain they worship Me, teaching as doctrines the commandments of men." (Mark 7:7). If we make our plans, have all sorts of programs without first of all praying and committing our way to the Lord, those plans and programs are without the needed power and authority of the risen Christ.

The apostle Paul forewarned us that in the latter days many would turn away from the true faith, wanting their ears tickled, not enduring sound doctrine. His warning is clear. Men will appear preaching another gospel. (1 Timothy 4:1, 2). When the primary commitment is to religious activity it makes null and void the needed intimacy that can bring true discipleship. It is Christ without a Cross.

The gospel offered by charlatans, another step away from the sound doctrine Paul spoke about, will be a perversion of the true gospel of Christ. They will invent a new Jesus. Right now, a false Christ is being preached even in some evangelical churches. Theirs is a Christ who calls for no repentance. It is a Christ who embraces homosexuality and same-sex marriage. It is also a Christ who accepts false religions in the name of love and tolerance. The teaching of *Chrislam* to appease the Muslim world in itself is a denial of Scripture. All part of a great falling away and deception foretold in God's Word.

We also find today a false theology that God does not punish those who have been redeemed. This false notion releases them from any responsibility and personal accountability for sin once they have been saved. The church and nation that professes their faith in God, but neglects to walk humbly and obediently to God's covenant, while expecting His blessings, are sadly mistaken. We are to keep short accounts with the Lord, working out our salvation with fear and trembling (Philippians 2:12). The writer of the book of Hebrews gives us light on the subject. (Hebrews 3:7).

The Church is the salt of the earth. Salt is a preservative. It holds back corruption and decay. The corruption comes in all forms. We see political corruption, moral corruption and social corruption. Jesus made it quite clear regarding the church. He said, "If the salt has lost its flavor, how shall it be seasoned? It is then good for nothing *but to be thrown out and trampled* underfoot by men." The integrity of America is in the hands of the true church. God is about to end the religious game many Americans are playing.

When the Church ceases to be the salt and light, corruption sets in. The powers of darkness have a great avenue in making inroads into every part of society. This is what we are experiencing in America today.

As the Church ceases to fulfill its true purpose it will continue to be trampled underfoot of men. As in the past, history revealed these men as communists, Nazis and many other *isms*. Today we see Islamism that has re-emerged and appears to be overtaking nations, and gaining great strongholds in America. As the Church remains complacent and compromising, not fulfilling its role as salt and light, men will continue to trample under their feet the church in America as they reach out with the hand of compromise and surrender to the truth of God's Word adhering to the vain traditions of men.

America is in desperate need of a spiritual awakening. It is not a time for murky messages, vague voices, or stammering sermons

We live in a fairy-tale existence that all is well. It can be said the unique blessings America has enjoyed have no doubt brought about pride and self-sufficiency. These two elements alone can be the root cause of the grave national crisis we now face as a nation. The prophet Malachi explained it this way: "If you do not hear, And if you will not take it to heart, To give glory to My name," says the Lord of hosts, "I will send a curse upon you, And I will curse your blessings. Yes, I have cursed them already, Because you do not take it to heart" (Malachi 2:2).

America and the world are fighting conflicts with sophisticated weapons. This is in fact the manifestation of what is taking place in the heavenlies. It is intense spiritual warfare for the souls of men and nations. A weakened and complacent church is blinded to the raging storms that assail our nation. Worldliness and false doctrines have neutralized the church. Warning judgments have been ignored as the church, rather than understanding the times, is misreading them.

The result of a church that has fallen far short of claiming, demonstrating and representing the authority of the risen Christ, no longer under His true authority, in spiritual reality, has no authority. Jesus speaks of this condition in churches today throughout our nation. His warning is toward those whose lives do not bear fruit.

The comforts of the American Church bring with it the deception that all is well: "We are triumphant and let us hear only good reports".

"I know your works, that you are neither cold nor hot. I could wish you were cold or hot. So then, because you are lukewarm, and neither cold nor hot, I will vomit you out of My mouth" (Revelation 3:15,16).

In the Old Testament we saw how the prophet Jeremiah dwelt among many false prophets who were leading the people astray. Through their messages they told the people they would not see famine or sword, but in the midst of everyone doing his own thing, following the ways of their own heart, they still would have peace. Many false visions, divinations and illusions have entered into the Church through false prophets and their dogmas as seen in Jeremiah:

"Because from the least of them even to the greatest of them, everyone is given to covetousness; And from the prophet even to the priest, Everyone deals falsely. They have also healed the hurt of my people slightly, Saying, Peace, peace!' When there is no peace" (Jeremiah 6:13,14).

WARNINGS FOR COMPLACENCY

The prophet Amos was given a message of warning to Israel; but first came the message of mercy. He knew Israel was at the door of judgment. And so Amos preached, " Thus saith the Lord...Seek ye me, and ye shall live... Seek the Lord...lest he break out like fire in the house of Joseph, and devour it, and there be none to quench it..." (Amos 5:4-6). Prosperous Israel did not repent of these warnings. The prophet was hated for the message he was giving. "They hate him that rebuketh in the gate, and they abhor him that speaketh uprightly" (vs. 10).

The American church lies in its comfort and complacency. Amos was telling Israel that your lifestyle will be shaken and disturbed, as they had lost their burden and purpose while being asleep in the light. They were comfortable and complacent. Christians who have no burden for the lost, live in their comfort and do not grieve over our nation's sins. They don't have time to listen to a "gloom and doom" message they see as negative, while missing the warning judgments of God. It's a picture of today's backslidden church. Not wanting to hear truth, the modern church is enjoying their prosperity too much to be disturbed and has become spiritually blinded to the dangers and the sword coming against America and the world.

However, Amos cried out, as His words ring true at this hour: "Woe to them that are at ease in Zion...that put far away the evil day...that lie upon beds of ivory, and stretch themselves upon their couches, and eat the lambs out of the flock...that chat to the sound of the viol...that drink wine in bowls, and anoint themselves with the chief ointments: but they are not grieved for the affliction of Joseph...Therefore those who recline at banquets shall be removed" (Amos 6:1-7).

Jesus Himself issued a sobering judgment against those who profess but do not possess true faith in God and follow their faith according to the Bible: "Not everyone that says, Lord, shall enter into the Kingdom of God... (Matthew 7:22).

The American church seems to think America won't be judged while standing on one single verse in the Bible: "If My people who are called by Name, shall humble themselves, and pray and seek my face, and turn from their wicked ways; then I will hear from heaven, and I will forgive their sin, and will heal their land." (2 Chronicles 7:14).

This is a verse in Scripture every prayer warrior and dedicated intercessor is familiar with. The question to be asked is; Where is the evidence that America has repented? What evidence do we see of our national leaders humbling themselves and turning from their wicked ways. The ways of our nation have become more wicked by the minute. From the White House to the masses, with a majority approving and agreeing with a president and his policies that openly violate the laws and statues of Almighty God, who trifles with the injunctions of morality, condoning and promoting perversion, while in brazen defiance swears on a Bible to uphold and protect the very foundations of freedom and liberty, along with the standard of righteousness laid out in scripture for the well-being and protection of the people. God's eternal laws and rules are openly being violated while many professing Christians have voted a man over the Bible. A great falling away what God commands and requires.

> God does not need a multitude of echoes from diluted, watered down man-pleasing messages. He needs a clear voice to be heard.

Is this the great apostasy the apostle Paul spoke about? "They have forsaken the right way and gone astray, following the way of Balaam the son of Beor, who loved the wages of unrighteousness; but he was rebuked for his iniquity; a dumb donkey speaking with a man's voice restrained him the madness of the prophet" (2 Peter 2:15-17).

God does not need a multitude of echoes from diluted, watered down man-pleasing messages in America. He needs a clear voice. It is time for a distinct, clear call to come forth. The words of the apostle Paul are for us today in this critical and crucial hour of history, "For if the trumpet gives and uncertain voice, who shall prepare himself for war?" (1 Corinthians 14:8).

Like it was for Israel of old, America is disobeying and quickly departing from God's laws...and like ancient Israel, the light and covenant given to them by God is being extinguished and forfeited.

Because America has not considered her God-given destiny in upholding His statues and judgments, which made her great, America will fall as did ancient Israel, and her collapse will be awesome.

"Jerusalem has sinned gravely,
Therefore she has become vile.
All who honored her despise her
Because they have seen her nakedness;
Yes, she sighs and turns away.

Her uncleanness is in her skirts;
She did not consider her destiny;
Therefore her collapse was awesome."
(Lamentations 1:8,9).

A FALLING AWAY

In the late 1800's, the Church in Europe failed to keep its focus on the cross of Christ and the promise of Christ's return. As a result it grew steadily "worldly" and cold. After generations of subtly departing from the Bible, the Church in Europe today is almost nonexistent. Rather than the light and authority of Jesus Christ, there are more Muslims in Europe today than true believers in Jesus Christ.

> The church in Europe has grown cold and vibrant faith has disappeared so that there are now more Muslims in Europe than true believers in Christ.

European countries one day will be worshipping a different God, namely, Allah. While Islam is having an explosion in population in Europe, the Europeans are making concessions to try and appease their Muslim population going as far as removing crucifixes in schools and hospitals as not to offend Muslims. Public funds are also being donated to build mosques.

In rejecting God's truth, the countries of Europe could very well be overtaken by cruel Islamic laws and will eventually have to conform to the heavy hand of intolerance that so many Europeans despise today. The official policy in America public squares is the cry for freedom *from* religion. This leaves the vacuum that Islam will not tolerate, a religion that encompasses the whole life and law of Muslims. Islam is a political system, an ideology, within a religious framework that controls all aspects of the Muslim life and desires that all will bow to the law of Islam, sooner than later.

The European Church failed to seize the moment. It is a wake-up call to the American Church in this final hour. As Islam invades North America, a religious and political force steadily taking more ground throughout the world. We are seeing the "perfect storm," a weakened Church in her comfort and complacency and an aggressive Islamic agenda spreading and raging throughout the world and within America.

While the Church in America took a different road than Europe, today powerful forces are eating away at her strength. Having its focus away from the cross and Jesus' second coming, the church has largely focused on wealth and materialism. Their focus is on this world and material gain and not the Lord's imminent return (Luke 21:34).

Scripture clearly tells us God's anger burned against ancient Israel. As it was, He delivered them into the hands of plunders who despoiled them; and, He sold them into the hands of their enemies all around, so they could no longer stand before their enemies. As we continue to insult God in every aspect of our society, we cannot claim that God is on our side in the war against terrorism and those who are in total opposition to our culture and the faith we claim that in reality has given us God's protection.

Sworn enemies from outside and within, playing on America's tolerance, freedom of religion, and civil and political rights,continue to deplete the strength she once had—as well as the respect throughout the world. America increasingly losing its influence in the world. This is the result of America's departing of her spiritual and moral laws and principles given to her from the Source that made her great.

These false doctrines have not only drawn away large numbers of Christians, but have weakened the Church in regard to the importance of Israel and our Judeo-Christian foundations which are eroding from within. The main target of both radical and moderate Islam is their determined goal to undermine and destroy both Israel and America.

Without salt corruption sets in. Many Christians are caught up in their everyday lives of materialism, pleasures, politics, etc., and cannot spiritually discern the lateness of the hour. They cannot understand the times. The *ism* that now is trampling down America, and the church through compromise and ignorance, the religion of Islam will eventually stifle our Judeo-Christian culture, especially if America continues to push and demand a two-state solution in Israel that would divide the land of Israel. God has already warned any nation who would try to divide His land will fall into the same judgment as other nations in history have. (Joel 2:20).

UNDERSTANDING THE TIMES

The Church needs to understand the times and urgency of the hour as never before. If America goes the way of its Islamic-friendly agenda, giving accommodation to an ideology totally opposed to the founding of our nation, it will be a great defeat for Judeo-Christianity and the liberty and freedom of our democracy at home and abroad.

Those nations that are sworn enemies of the values, faith and culture that have made America the beacon of Christianity, a safe haven for the Jewish people, with liberty and freedom for all; now with a great falling away from the foundations of those truths, an exhausted military, an unstable economy and a weakening dollar, America is now in a period of its history of diminishing from a nation, the American age, we once knew.

The church must have the cry of Mordecai. It must be clear, it must be consistent and it must be loud enough to sound the alarm of the dangers that now threaten are very existence. The church also must become like the sons of Issachar, who "understood the times, and knew what (Israel) should do (1 Chronicles 12: 32).

America and the world have entered into the most challenging and critical time in history. People are alarmed as they see dramatic and fearful events on every front. Many are seeking, through many different avenues, insights into what the future holds. Jesus warned, "That even the elect would be deceived…if it were possible." If the body of Christ does not arise and boldly declare with a clear prophetic voice, the people will continue to turn to the darkness of the occult and new age seers.

The question of Mordecai to Esther is the question for us in this crucial hour: "If you keep quiet at a time like this, God will deliver the Jews from some other source, but you and your relatives will die; What's more, who can say but that God has brought you into the palace (America) for such a time as this? (Esther 4:14).

We, as the body of Christ need to arise from our spiritual slumber and begin to let the light of the Gospel be seen in America. The Word of the Lord from Isaiah 60:1 is for the Church today: "Arise and shine, for the glory of the Lord is risen upon thee".

And, we must become like Esther, who finally understood the reason for her being in a royal position. She could no longer remain silent. Her life was in the same danger as her people. "For who knows that you have come to the kingdom for such a time as this. And if you remain silent deliverance will come from some other source…" (Esther 4:14). There remains no other source but the Church.

The Church in the same position and danger as was Esther. The spirit of Haman is raging through Islam to subjugate all mankind to the law of Islam, along with Islamic firebrands who are about to wield nuclear weapons. The weapon in the church's battle to succeed is to be armed with the Word of God, prayer and the right attitude in becoming effective in engaging within American society. Having a good conscience; that, whereas they speak evil of you, as evildoers, they may be ashamed that falsely accuse your conversation in Christ. "For it is better, if the will of God be so, that you suffer for well doing, than for evil doing" (1 Peter 3:16,17).

We need to be a people of courage without compromise, throwing off the sins of comfort and complacency, and the sin that so easily besets us, willing to stand for truth no matter what the cost. The times demand it.

We read in Matthew 3:8 where the disciple John was speaking to the Pharisees and Sadducees who came to his baptism. This compares to the religious crowd and leaders of our day. John had warned them to "flee from the wrath to come" declaring to them, "Bring forth therefore fruits meet for repentance. And think not to say within yourselves, We have Abraham to our father....." (Matthew 3:8-9).

Religious traditions, church affiliation and membership do not place us in right standing with God. An attitude of spiritual pride is a stench in the nostrils of a holy God. "Who say, 'Keep to yourself, do not come near me, For I am holier than you! These are smoke in My nostrils, A fire that burns all day." (Isaiah 65:5)

Humanism, arrogance and spiritual pride separate us from God, neither can we meet God's requirements for true repentance found in 2 Chronicles 7:14. Pride is in complete contrast to the *key* requirement which is humility.

Over the last few decades the church has been attacked on many fronts: from the liberal media to universities, that have been hostile to the Christian faith.

It has dramatically impacted the generation of today. We now see our own government turning its power and influence against Bible believers. The very attack comes from those, including our government, that desire to control the lives and behaviors of its citizens. It is the government's desire to undo the Judeo-Christian foundations that America was founded on. It is a strategy to move America toward greater if not total human secularism and dependence upon the government.

Meanwhile, the media in America, which purposely and systematically makes every effort to silence and deny the Christian voice, is at the same time elevating and promoting the "peaceful" religion of Islam. With every excuse they justify Muslim extremism while condemning and discarding the Christian foundations of faith and our very culture that has given America true liberty and freedom. Yet, many compromise and sympathize with Islam, wanting to appease and join hands in the name of peace, forgetting that Jesus Christ is the way, the truth and the life. "There is no other name given under heaven by which man may be saved" (Acts 4:12).

God gave his solemn assessment of the human unity He observed at the tower of Babel and said: "Behold, they are one people, and they all have the same language. And this is what they began to do, and now nothing which they purpose to do will be impossible for them" (Genesis 11:6, NASB).

It is not difficult to think of the power of human endeavor when those involved were united in one effort, even in rebellion against God. When we observe this incredible power of human unity we must then think of the awesome power that our spiritual unity can produce through the power of the Holy Spirit to bring true revival to our nation.

With a church active and empowered by God's Spirit we can witness a power not only to change our nation but to frustrate the plans of every evil agenda that desires our destruction. One nation under God would become a powerful spiritual force that God intended. Jesus said, *"I will build My church and the gates of hell shall not prevail against it"* (Matthew 16:18b, KJV).

We need the power of God to fall and when it does all other things will be insignificant in light of God's glory.

"Arise, shine; For your light has come! And the glory of the Lord is risen upon you. For behold, the darkness shall cover the earth, And deep darkness the people; But the Lord will arise over you. The Gentiles shall come to your light, And kings to the brightness of your rising" (Isaiah 60:1-3).

Religious piety and pride has no place when the reality of the gospel exposes it for what it is. Mere religion and pious pretense cannot mix with truth. When God's Word is preached without compromise and applied directly to the hearts of the people, it convicts men of their sin. Religion and truth cannot sit at the same table. Religion will change your mind, but it can never change your heart (John 3:3). We need the power of God to fall and when it does all other things will be insignificant in light of God's glory.

Dr. Erwin Lutzer of Moody Church in Chicago said this:

It's popular to blame the Supreme Court, the humanists, and radical feminists for our country's eroding standards of decency and growing disrespect for human life. But the responsibility might more properly be laid at the feet of those who know the living God but have failed to influence society.

If we were few in number, we might evade the blame, but there are tens of thousands of evangelical congregations and several million born-again believers in America. Yet we continue to lose critical battles. *Perhaps the church doesn't suffer for the sins of the world as much as the world suffers for the sins of the church.*

AMERICA & GOD'S EVERLASTING COVENANT

The entire history of the Old Testament is the history of one nation, that nation being Israel. Other nations enter the story only when they connect with Israel. They connect either in battle or in their forming alliances. The nation of Israel had a covenant with God. We find God's heart in regard to His chosen people. And because Israel had a unique relationship with God, the nation was more accountable and was judged more severely as a result of the light given and relationship they had with God. To whom much is given, much will be required.

In the late 1800's, God was bringing back the Jews through the Zionist movement. World War I and II saw the allied powers defeat the axis powers. Through America's defeating Hitler and coming into an alliance with the nation of Israel it has brought untold blessings to America. History reveals that as God was bringing the Jews back into their homeland after being scattered for thousands of years, He was raising up America at the exact time as a world power.

President Harry S. Truman held office during the end of World War II. America had just come through a decade in which evil forces, namely Nazi Germany and her allies, lined up in a bitter fight to banish religion and democracy from the face of the earth. President Truman's determination to recognize Israel as a modern state was a result of his lifelong belief that in the book of Genesis, God had given the land of Israel to the Jewish people for all time (Genesis 13:15).

God greatly used America in His plan for the Jewish people and the nation of Israel. America was the nation in time and history that welcomed the Jews with open arms becoming a safe haven as they escaped from the horrors of Nazism.

The rebirth of Israel was the greatest prophetic miracle of our day. It was only 60 plus years ago, May 14, 1948, that Israel was declared a nation. The prophet Isaiah foretold 2,500 years ago this great event would take place in the latter days. Israel was a chosen nation by God only on the fact that it was His sovereign choosing. The Bible tells us that the earth is the Lord's to do with as He wills (Psalm 24:1; Exodus 19:5).

We read of God's choice of the Jews in Genesis 17:8 where He declared the people of Israel holy, chosen to be "a people for Himself, a special treasure above all the peoples on the face of the earth." He picked the Jewish nation. They are an example of God's goodness and sever-ity, and to all who profess, "In God We Trust," those hav-ing knowledge of His statues and judgments.

For us to understand God's prophetic time clock and the season of history we are now living in, we must turn our focus on His prophetic plan for Israel. Without seeing the cohesiveness of His plan and purpose concerning Israel and the anti-Semitism again emerging, we are blinded to see what now looms on the horizon and what has clearly been prophesied (Zechariah 12:3).

SHARED VALUES & TRADITIONS

It was America that cooperated with God's agenda for the nation of Israel. God was working in a mighty way through the restoration of the Jewish nation, using America as her greatest ally and protector. It was America that made Israel the greatest military power in the Middle East to the dismay of her Arab-Muslim neighbors. One of the key reasons God has favored and blessed America can be in the fact of its Judeo-Christian foundations that were derived from the Jewish nation. Along with our shared values and traditions, our ongoing relationship has only cemented the two democracies together. Both the moral and legal codes that govern both nations were established under Judeo-Christian principles and faith.

America has shared a special 60 plus year alliance with Israel. America is not God's chosen nation: Israel was God's chosen nation and established by God. It was through the Jewish nation and its patriarchs' who proclaimed the moral and spiritual laws and principles of God that set the standard of righteousness for America, and those nations that were founded on Judeo-Christian principles. The Old Testament from the Book of Genesis to the Book of Deuteronomy is the Jewish Torah.

President Harry S. Truman after World War II boldly supported the creation of a Jewish homeland after Hitler's Nazi regime murdered over six million Jews. He reminded Americans in his 1946 speech of what America fought for and how to preserve it. Truman said:

"We have just come through a decade in which forces of evil in various parts of the world have been lined up in a bitter fight to banish from the face of the earth…religion and democracy.

President Truman went on to say:

"If men and nations would but live by the precepts of the ancient prophets and the teachings of the Sermon on the Mount, problems which now seem so difficult would soon disappear… This is a supreme opportunity for the Church to continue to fulfill its mission on earth…Oh, for an Isaiah or a Saint Paul to reawaken this sick world to its moral responsibilities!"

America is dangerously close to going the way other nations have gone in respect to Israel and interfering with the covenant God established with Israel. Not only is America falling away from her Judeo-Christian foundations and faith, her Mideast policies that now demand Israel to divide Jerusalem with her Arab Muslim enemies will negate God's sure promise of His blessings and protection on America. America has done much to destabilize Israel and has already triggered God's judgments. The Bible clearly gives warning in regard to God's chosen people and the nation of Israel:

"I will bless those who bless you and curse those who curse *(treat you with contempt)*. All families on earth will be blessed through you" (Genesis 12:3).

With America, turning away from her very source of blessing, abandoning her Judeo-Christian values while compromising those values in appeasing the Islamic world, who are determined to undermine and destroy western culture, with the goal in mind to subjugate the world for Allah, is nothing short of a recipe for disaster.

The false doctrines of dominion and replacement theology along with revisionist history has blinded America to the significance of Israel and God's warning judgments.

There continues to be a bitter fight to banish religion and democracy from the face of the earth. The most dangerous of all is the bitter fight within America to banish God from all sectors of society. Along with America's apostasy and appeasement to the enemies of our Judeo-Christian foundations, it will diminish America as a world-power bringing with it deadly consequences. In the end it will be the undoing and demise of a great nation once blessed by the God.

There is a definite clash of cultures in the age we are now living in. Without the standard of righteousness being raised and the acknowledgement of God we are destined to be undermined and stand to become the victim and not the victor in this cultural, political, and spiritual war.

PROGRESSIVE JUDGMENTS

In the past two decades America has experienced God's righteous indignation and His progressive judgments on every occasion America has pressured and demanded Israel give up her land (Joel 3: 2).

America which used to boast in her Christian founding principles, and her Judeo-Christian faith and foundations that have shaped Americas' culture would do well to keep forefront the spiritual heritage and her special alliance with Israel, her greatest ally and only democracy in the Middle East. America is dangerously close to going the way other nations have gone in respect to their treatment of Israel and interfering with the covenant God established with Israel. The Jewish nation was a sovereign act of God (Ezekiel 5:5).

One of the clearest messages contained in scripture is found in the book of Genesis. God gives a promise to those that bless Israel, they too will be blessed. On the flip side is the promise that those who curse Israel will themselves be cursed. (Genesis 12:3). The truth of this scripture is also repeated in Deuteronomy 28:7, Isaiah 41:10-12; Jeremiah 10:25 and Micah 5:9.

God has reserved a terrible judgment upon those who ignore His gift of the land to Jacob's seed..."I will seek to destroy all nations that come against Jerusalem" (Zechariah 12:2-9). America is without exception.

America's Mideast policies since 1991 have seriously undermined the long established and special relationship America holds with Israel. America began to wane in October 1991 as it began to directly interfere with God's prophetic plan for Israel in pressuring Israel to give up her land for peace with her Muslim neighbors, sworn enemies of Israel. As America initiated the Madrid Peace Treaty in Madrid, Spain, under President George Bush Sr. From that date on an intensity of natural disasters followed each time America began to pressure Israel to give land for peace with those seeking her destruction.

History reveals those nations that have incurred the righteous judgment of God on those who cursed the Jews.

Near the close of 2001, America experienced its greatest surprise attack since Pearl Harbor. It was September 11, 2001. America, under President George Bush Jr., again pressured Israel to retreat to indefensible pre-1967 Six-Day War borders in August 2001, which would be a formula for war and would interfere with God's prophetic plan for Israel. The horrific disaster finished off the decade. Ongoing devastation and disasters continued through the second decade (2001-2011). In every disaster it was always at the time America was demanding of Israel to give up covenant land (*Israel: A Cup of Drunkenness to the Nations; Bruce W. Assaf; Essence Books*).

Nearing the end of 2011, president Barack Hussein Obama pressured and demanded that Israel be divided weeks before the 10th anniversary of 9/11. A powerful earthquake shook Washington, D.C. as a series of violent storm activity that followed Hurricane Irene swept destructive forces in its wake. The forces of Hurricane Irene and the earthquake cracked the Washington Monument, led to the evacuation of the Pentagon, and made the Washington National Cathedral unusable. Called "an act of God" all these natural disasters happened at the exact same time America again demanded Israel to give up and divide east Jerusalem.

The Obama administration has proved to be the most anti-Semitic administration in Americas' history. The U.S. president has signaled to Israel that she is now on her own. And, as the first sitting U.S. president to publicly demand Israel to give up covenant land, it is in reality an outright defiance to the God of the Bible.

Americas' diplomatic strategy is more than technical shifts in their Mideast policies. It reflects in reality a total shift in values that ignores, dismisses and lays aside the very Judeo-Christian foundations of faith and culture that has brought God's blessings upon America. It is not only weakening those foundations, it now puts America in a position of God's indignation and righteous judgment (Genesis 12:3). It is God who owns the land rights on Israel and whoever touches Israel touches the apple of

God's eye arousing His jealous and righteous indignation (Leviticus 25:23).

America's cooling off and departing from its Judeo-Christian heritage now has chosen tolerance, appeasement and understanding toward America's enemies who seek not only Israel's destruction but America's. America now within a humanistic bubble, with its secular humanistic world view, makes excuses for evil, or worse, denies evil exists. Rather, evil is coddled by a refusal to confront it through appeasement of sworn enemies. The nation that wanted change without God is now a nation deceived and in danger of greater forthcoming judgments, the most dangerous of all, favoring the enemies of our very foundations, faith and culture who are determined in destroying the West.

> The greatest threat to the Holy Land is not only Islamic enemies, but America's new Mideast policies that are bargaining away Jerusalem, the City of the great King (Matthew 5:35).

We are indebted to Israel for the spiritual heritage we have received. With that inheritance Israel gave America and the world the Ten Commandments and brought our Lord and Savior into the world. Our political leaders must never forget this special alliance and spiritual bond. To disregard our spiritual heritage is in definition an open defiance and rebellion against the God of the Bible, the God of Abraham, Isaac and Jacob. It will invite the sure wrath and righteous indignation of Almighty God according to His unchanging word (Joel 3:2).

INEVITABLE JUDGEMENT

It was Harry S. Truman who faced his greatest challenge in his presidency over whether to support the creation of a Jewish homeland in Palestine after World War II. On the eve of the British withdrawal, most American experts strongly opposed the creation of a Jewish state. President Truman solidified the newly formed nation of Israel that the hopes of the Jewish people became a reality. In his presidency Truman said:

> *"The fundamental basis of this nation's laws was given to Moses on the Mount. The fundamental basis of our Bill of Rights comes from the teaching we get from Exodus and Saint Matthew, from Isaiah and Saint Paul...If we don't have a proper fundamental moral background, we will finally end with a totalitarian government which does not believe in rights for anyone except the State!"*

The great falling away of America in its headlong rush to abandon God is charting a course down a dangerous path ignoring a warning from God on any nation who strives against His covenant land and people. "I will bless those that bless thee (Israel), and I will curse those that curse thee (Israel) (Genesis 12:3).

Everything falls into line in regard to God's everlasting covenant and our obedience in obeying and upholding God's laws. Departing from God's covenant in regard to Israel will bring about certain and swift judgments as God's Word says.

✝ America's alliance with Israel is our strongest line of defense. Our Homeland Security Director is the God of Abraham, Isaac and Jacob, the God of Israel who neither slumbers nor sleeps in regard to His land and His chosen people. America must understand the dire consequences of turning away from Israel and God's everlasting covenant.

A misguided administration who believes to appease the enemies of our faith and culture is driving America into committing judgment provoking sins targeted against Christians and the nation of Israel.

These events since 1991 have brought God's progressive judgment on America, and if America continues its pressure and withdraws its support of Israel, appeasing the Arab Muslim world, it could be a further cause of the demise of America as a leading nation in these perilous times and latter days of history.

America is the last supporter of an ever-increasing anti-Semitic world. In America's cooling off with its relationship with Israel all the stops will be pulled out. If America does not relent with its demand for Israel to divide (God's land) their land, America will be listed with those nations who have experienced the hot displeasure of God. The permanence of the nation of Israel and His blessings and curses upon those who violate His covenant is clearly described in scripture and points out their final end:

"I will also gather all nations, and will bring them down into the valley of Jehoshaphat, and will judge them there for my people, and for my heritage, Israel, whom they have scattered among the nations and **parted my land**" (Joel 3:2). Emphasis added. America now stands on the verge of this inevitable judgment for all who divide the nation of Israel.

WARNING FROM HISTORY

Today, huge numbers of believers have become dead to God's prophetic plan. With a widespread lack of preaching and teaching regarding the cross of Christ and the Lord's soon coming, the false doctrine of replacement theology in regard to the nation of Israel, which says God has set aside Israel, has led directly to both spiritual decay and slumber within the church. Replacement theology has undermined the blessed hope that the church is keeping watchful and waiting for the Lord's soon return. Israel is God's signpost as latter day prophecies are being fulfilled now that the Jews are back in the land after thousands of years (Isaiah 66:8).

Israel is not only God's decisive issue to judge the nations but God's timepiece and prelude to His coming. The Bible clearly tells us the Gentiles are the engrafted vine. Israel was and is the natural vine. And although God scattered His people, He also declared that in the latter days, when the *"times of the Gentiles"* would be fulfilled, He would again bring back into the land His covenant people. We are now living on the other side of *the times of the Gentiles (Luke 21:24).*

With America undermining God's covenant and covenant land, appeasement of Islamic enemies will bring greater Muslim darkness over the Middle East and the world. Churchill declared to the nations in Europe as Hitler's Nazis were on their plight to defeat Britain and control the world: *"The lights in Europe are going out."* Churchill can be equated as a type of Mordecai. His cry to America almost fell on deaf ears if not for the attack on Pearl Harbor that awakened America to her enemies.

During this defining moment in world and America's history, America is dangerously close of going the way other nations have gone and are now going in their relationship with Israel.

September 11, 2001 brought to our attention the ideology of (radical Islam) like that of Hitler in its attempt to diminish and destroy our nation and all that America stands for. Hitler's tactical fabrication, saying a lie loud enough and long enough eventually penetrates as truth,was aimed at the Arab world for the destruction of the Jewish people in World War II. It continues today with America being deceived through its appeasement to the Islamic world.

With Muslim darkness sweeping the world the (Obama administration) has crafted policies, with a dangerous Islamic friendly agenda that destabilizes Israel bringing her to the brink of destruction from its Muslim enemies determined to destroy and control the Jewish homeland. It in turn will bring God's judgment upon America (Genesis 12:3).

When ancient Israel turned away from God's statues and judgments the Jews were scattered and suffered like no other race. They did not consider God's covenant and their God-given destiny.

The Book of Lamentations is Jeremiah's heart-cry over the terrible conditions that fell upon Judah after God fulfilled His word of judgment. It is an account written by the prophet how Jerusalem was besieged and destroyed. The temple was burned to the ground as the nation fell into utter sorrow and misery. Jerusalem was a jewel in the world's eyes, yet it came to total servitude to heathen enemies. These people were full of wickedness and rebellion, and they were still God's children, yet the Lord seemed to have little trouble judging them or even burning down His own temple. Scripture reminds us of the goodness and severity of a holy God.

God used wicked nations to judge His people who had knowledge of His covenant, His laws and statutes.

Ancient Israel was overrun by cruel foreigners who were instruments of God's righteous judgment. The Book of Lamentations spells out clearly how God dealt with the people He had chosen to establish His covenant. How much more severely those who have been acquainted with God's laws and statues:

"Jerusalem has sinned gravely, therefore she has become vile. All who honored her despise her because they have seen her nakedness; Yes, she sighs and turns away. Her uncleanness is in her skirts; She did not consider her destiny; *Therefore her collapse was awesome."* (Lamentations 1:8, 9).

History recounts how quickly a nation can disintegrate under divine judgment. As you prayerfully study Lamentations, it is clearly seen how severely God "… afflict(s)…for a multitude of…transgressions" (vs. 5). The same judgments that fell on Jerusalem are about to come upon America.

Because Israel enjoyed greater light and was more privileged, her judgment was to be more severe. Ancient Israel was a chosen nation. She knew God's laws therefore, her sin was greater. America has known God's laws and has been a privileged nation. America's outward piety professing her trust in God mixed with idolatry and now a turning away. If God caused an awesome collapse to a nation He chose to establish His covenant, having their God-given destiny in knowing and being familiar with His statues and judgments, why would He not judge America, as it has been given the same light and opportunity to be a blessed nation.

America now stands to suffer the same fate, both having common enemies and both being raised up from nothing has been given great light. Israel was a nation chosen of God with an everlasting covenant. Unless our government and people come to a place of national repentance, we too will see the awesome collapse of our nation, especially in light of America's treatment in regard to Israel in this hour of history. As other nations in history, God knows their plans. The plans president Obama is to direct policies concerning Israel to the United Nations, which is pro-Arab and against Israel.

"They have taken crafty counsel against thy people... they have said, come and let us cut them off from being a nation; that the name of Israel may be no more in remembrance." (Psalm 83:3, 4).

This is the great falling away of America, and the world, from the only true God. To be in opposition to Israel is in reality to being in opposition God. It is an open defiance of God Himself.

Man's rebellion and apostasy will accelerate end time events as He will soon gather the nations for judgment. To ignore Israel is to make every effort to eradicate God.

As many nations are mentioned in scripture in regard to the latter days,there is no mention of America. Yet, America' unique biblical heritage and her stature in the world would have us think America would be included as a major world power. It will be the result of America's turning away as Israel's greatest ally in the Middle East. *(Behind the Veil of Radical Islam: The Coming War, Bruce W. Assaf, Essence Books)*

America has been a safe harbour for the Jewish people. Making up over 3 percent of America's total population, Jewish people have been protected from harassment and anti-Semitism. America has given Jews great opportunities for educational, economics and cultural advancement while maintaining their religious freedom and identity. America has also been a beacon for Christianity.

Increasingly, in America there will be greater Islamic pressure and takeover placing America in great peril. America's stand affects the entire world. As the acknowledged leader of the free world, any U.S. president following a Muslim ideology and spurning its special alliance with Israel is setting a very dangerous precedent. Islamic darkness from without and now from within has been given a green light through naive and dangerous policies under the Obama administration. America's fatal mistake.

America is seeing the inevitable consequences of disobedience by playing into the hands of her enemies.

"Israel was holiness to the Lord, the firstfruits of His increase. All that devour him will offend; disaster will come upon them," says the Lord (Jeremiah 2:3).

As America supports Egypt's new government, namely the Muslim Brotherhood, sworn enemies of Israel, what does the near future hold as America pours millions of dollars into an Arab nation that openly declares by its new president, "Jerusalem is our goal. We shall pray in Jerusalem, or die as martyrs in its threshold." The determined goal of the Arab Muslim world is to defeat Israel, and all other western democracies. The bitter fight to destroy religion and democracy is being aided by America's own president and administration. Is this the deception America finds herself in as a result of her backsliding and departure from God?

Now with America falling away, history will repeat itself. Blindness to the significance of the nation of Israel, replacement theology and revisionist history brings with it dangerous compromise, spiritual weakness and decay, and a clouding over of what now looms on the horizon for America and the world. God's righteous judgment for all who turn from Israel, and the rejection of salvation God has offered and given to the world.

The great apostasy of America and the world is the beginning of latter day prophecies being fulfilled. These prophecies could not begin to unfold and be fulfilled until Israel was brought back into the land. (Ezekiel 37, 38 & 39).

CLEAR WARNING

America cannot take God into its battles expecting Him to win them on our behalf. There can be no doubt that God has blessed America. Even though God is not an American, or any other nationality, we can be encouraged to know that the founding and development of the American republic is legendary. As we read the founding documents and take a tour of America's historical monuments, it all reveals to us a deep awareness of the God of the Bible.

The underpinnings of America are Bible based. When the first settlers arrived in America, their influence of the Bible came with them. Their Christian faith was as much part of them as was their determination and bravery. The Rhode Island Charter of 1683, pointed out clearly what these individual colonies reflected. Their statements reflected the goal of their government:

> *"We submit our person, lives, and estates unto our Lord Jesus Christ, the King of kings and Lord of lords, and to all those perfect and most absolute laws of His given us in His Holy Word."* The Bible was considered the rule of life in the colonies.

As a result of a once God-fearing beginning, America experienced the blessings on God: "If you fully obey the Lord your God by keeping all the commands I am giving you today, the Lord your God will exalt you above all nations of the world. You will experience all these blessings if you obey the voice of the Lord" (Deuteronomy 28:1-2).

As America foolishly departs from the Living God, the blessings and exaltation of America bestowed upon her, is now in this time of her history proving otherwise. America's behavior is now negating her world power status and influence with her once great blessings being forfeited.

The real question to ask is are we on God's side? While God is our greatest hope and source of blessings in all aspects of life, He is also our greatest threat.

Ronald Reagan, the 40th U.S. president stated, *"America was founded by people who believe(d) that God was their rock of safety. I recognize that we must be cautious in claiming God is on our side, but I think it's all right to keep asking if we are on God's side."*

No nation, however, can claim that God is on its side. Israel was the only nation that God made an everlasting covenant with long ago.

America's abandoning of her values and the light given her has obviously brought waves of progressive judgment. The Book of Lamentations tells us: "Like a widow broken with grief she sits alone in her mourning. She, once queen of nations, is now a slave. She sobs through the night;

tears run down her cheeks. Among all her lovers, there is none to help her. All her friends are now her enemies" (Lamentations. 1:1-2).

We read from the book of Job: "With Him are strength and prudence. The deceived and the deceiver are His. He leads counselors away plundered, And makes fools out of judges. He loosens the bonds of kings, And binds and binds their waists with a belt, He leads princes away plundered, And overthrows the mighty...*He makes nations great, and destroys them; he enlarges nations, and* guides them. He takes away the understanding of the chiefs of the people of the earth, And makes them wander in a pathless wilderness" (Job 12:17-24).

We cannot alter the fact that America has done much good and has done more things right in the building of our nation. Biblical principles and an acknowledgment of God over the years have given moral and spiritual values to our nation. However, God's Word brings to light and gives America clear warning and clarity regarding any people and nation revealing the goodness and severity of God. Scripture tells us His righteous judgment and indignation for all who despise and forsake His judgments and statues:

"The instant I speak concerning a nation and concerning a kingdom, to pluck up, to pull down, and to destroy it, if that nation against whom I have spoken turns from it's evil, I will relent of the disaster that I thought to bring upon it.

"And the instant I speak concerning a nation and concerning a kingdom, to build and to plant it, if it does evil in My sight so that it does not obey My voice, then I will relent concerning the good with which I said I would benefit it...."Thus says the Lord: "Behold, I am fashioning a disaster and a devising a plan against you. Return now everyone from his evil way, and make your ways and your doings good,' " (Jeremiah 18:9-11).

RENDERING OUR HEARTS

"Now, therefore," says the Lord, "Turn to Me with all your heart, With fasting, with weeping, and with mourning. "So rend your heart, and not your garments; return to the Lord your God, For He is gracious and merciful, Slow to anger, and of great kindness; And he relents from doing harm. Who knows if he will turn and relent, And a leave a blessing behind Him" (Joel 2:12-14).

God was saying through His prophet, "Rend your hearts, and not your garments." In other words religious activity and lip service is not enough, and never can be, especially in what you are seeing happening to you and your nation: "turn ye even to me with all your heart, and with fasting, and with weeping, and with mourning: And rend your heart and not your garments, and turn unto the Lord your God…" (Joel 2:12-13).

Many think fasting is not eating. When we fast it is more than just refraining from food. It is breaking away from the norm, turning from habits and ways displeasing to God and humbling ourselves before God putting away all distractions. It is a time when we make our hearts open to receive and hear from God, clearing the pathway of our heart to hear and receive from God.

It is a time of genuine sorrow for the sins we have committed and going to the Lord in repentance and sincerity of heart. God desires and requires for us to live in holiness, without it the scripture says, no man shall see the Lord.

No longer can we as the church give God mere lip service. It is a time and hour when we need to render our hearts and not our garments. The prophet Joel was God's voice to the children of Israel at a time Israel was facing their greatest natural disaster(s) that had come upon the nation.

There was a drought throughout the land. The land lay parched as a result of this great drought. The pastures were destroyed where livestock grazed, along with an invasion of locust as both vines and fig trees were destroyed.

In Joel's day the prophet saw the devastation as a judgment of God for the sin that the nation of Israel had committed in the land.

Today in America we see the same drought and famine in our land in the form of weather pattern changes, droughts, floods, hurricanes, tornadoes along with economic woes and the ever increasing destructive habits of sin; drug and alcohol abuse, abortion, homosexuality, political greed, corruption and deception within our government, and the list goes on.

The Jews in the Old Testament tore their garments. The word 'rend' means to 'separate through force or violence'. Their custom of the day when fasting was to tear their garments and then clothe themselves with sackcloth.

They would sprinkle ashes on their head as an outward sign of mourning and sorrow for their sins. It was possible for them to just render their garments and not their hearts, the outward motion of religious tradition.

When we render our hearts to a loving, gracious and merciful heavenly Father, we will begin to experience again the purity of heart that allows God's very presence and power to flow freely in and through us. It is then, and only then, we place ourselves in a position to intercede for our nation, our loved ones, the lost, having full confidence that God is not only hearing our prayers, but is actively at work answering our prayers (Isaiah 65:24).

SUPERFICIAL REVIVAL

After one of the worst periods of history, ancient Israel experienced a superficial revival. When Manasseh ruled Israel, the Bible tells us he was declared the most wicked king in the nations entire history: "…Manasseh seduced them to do more evil than did the nations whom the Lord destroyed before the children of Israel" (2 Kings 21:9).

The evil found in the nation of Israel was even worse than that of the surrounding heathen nations. America professing "In God We Trust" continues to openly defy the God of the Bible and has become more violent and wicked than surrounding nations, given the light and grace shed upon her. As perversion and the shedding of innocent blood is endorsed by the highest office in the land, how that America's president, swearing an oath on God's Word, (Abraham Lincoln's Bible) has blatantly disregarded the statues and judgments of God, in light of Lincoln's prayer, a president who was in a holy fear and reverence of God when he had prayed in the midst of a war-torn nation:

> *"It is the duty of all nations as well as of men to own their dependence upon the overruling power of God, to confess their sins and transgressions in humble sorrow*

yet with assured hope that genuine repentance will lead to mercy and pardon, and to recognize the sublime truth, announced in the Holy Scriptures and proven by all history: that those nations only are blessed whose God is the Lord..." Abraham Lincoln

In this perilous hour of history there appears to be no thought or inclination to humbly seek God and repent of our outright pride and arrogance. This rebellion and deception is further removing America from God's requirements and laws, and sadly and tragically spurning His grace and mercy. This hollow hypocrisy will surely provoke a holy God for greater judgments to fall. "Woe be to them that call evil good, and good evil" (Isaiah 5).

Manasseh did more to bring God's anger and wrath on Israel than any other king. : "... Moreover Manasseh shed innocent blood very much, till he had filled Jerusalem from one end to another...provoking God to anger..." (vs. 16). If we are honest and intimate with the God of the Bible, we can put America, along with (the president), who holds the highest office in the land in place of Manasseh and his deeds of rebellion against God. Yet, God is not mocked. Listen to what God says:

..."Behold, I am bringing such evil upon Jerusalem and Judah, that whosoever hearth of it, both his ears shall tingle...and I will wipe out Jerusalem as a man wipeth a dish, wiping it, and turning it upside down (Verse 12-13). God had enough with Jerusalem and was headed for judgment because of Manasseh's evil. Has God had enough with America?

Surprisingly, God raised up a righteous man and a holy remnant in Jerusalem after Manasseh. It was King Josiah and his court. Josiah saw the evil and decided to begin a purge. He tore down the houses of prostitution and sodomy, and slew all the temple prostitutes. Those of the occult, the priests and the priestess were killed and their shrines destroyed. He broke all the idols into pieces and even went as far as burning human bones on the shrines' altars. This signified that they were desecrated forever.

There was great reformation in Israel's laws and government as he sent out godly teachers in calling the people back to God. The scriptures were lying dormant for years in the temple when they were found by a priest who brought them back to Josiah and read them aloud to him. Josiah, after legislating holiness, began reading God's holy word, fell on his face in anguish.

What did Josiah hear to drop to his knees and anguish? He heard Moses command to Israel, laid out plainly in Deuteronomy: " Ye shall walk after the Lord your God, and fear Him, and keep His commandments, and obey His voice, and ye shall serve Him, and cleave unto Him" (Deuteronomy 13:4). Josiah also heard the prophecy from Jeremiah: "… (Israel) has a whore's forehead, thou refusedth to be ashamed" (Jeremiah 3:3).

Yet, in the midst of one of the greatest reformations in the history of ancient Israel, Josiah's heart was smitten in hearing God's word and seeing little of it had touched the people's heart. He saw it didn't matter whether he cleaned up the nation outwardly, legislating holiness throughout the land. The curse of Deuteronomy would fall on the land.

America has thrown God's commandments far away from the public square and throughout its society. Rather than attempt any efforts and legislate laws to thwart the rising political and social power of militant homosexuals, to legislate against the bloodshed of abortion, outlaw pornography and gambling, and reinstall prayer into our schools and courts, along with purging America from drugs, murders and violence rampant across our nation, America has defiantly promoted and embraced wickedness, and having abolished God's law continue to profess "In God We Trust." This is more than hypocrisy. America has been blinded with deception is already being given over to a powerful delusion of believing God is in her midst. How terrible and frightening. America is past the tipping point!

America is going to be humbled. The judgments that are now falling are going to last a long time and increase if America does not turn back to God. Like past nations who refused to acknowledge the Lord, God's righteous indignation will sweep the land in a whirlwind of God's wrath with none to appease and help. Hurricane Sandy, along with many natural disasters, are examples of a waves of destruction never thought possible.

REPENTANCE, RESTORATION & REVIVAL

As we see the spiritual, moral and social decay that engulfs us, we know deep down something needs to change. Revival is the term used for to awaken, to make alive again. It tells us we need to return to something we have had in the past. Yet, what did we have in the past? If it was genuine and not the superficial, why would we need to return to something that needed reviving again? If that which we had died, was it the real thing to begin with. Too many times has there been a revival for the wrong reasons. Pleasant memories of something we had desires us to return or go back. Therefore, it is something we want, and is self-serving or superficial.

King Josiah discovered what appeared to be an effective revival, or reformation, but it was not deep enough in cutting to the heart of outward piety and pretense. It was merely lip service and something without inner depth that would change the people. True repentance will bring about restoration, and restoration in a man's soul will have him to become revived. That kind of change in the Bible is called repentance, which brings about true fruit and change in one's life.

Our willingness and confession of sin asking God 's forgiveness and grace to turn away from our own ways, our wicked ways, sinful desires, selfish ambitions, immoral life-styles of secret sins, greed, covetousness, unbelief and our compromise with the world will bring the needed blessings and favor of God back into our lives. We must bring and confess every known attitude and sin along with those ungodly ways we know is contrary to what is godly.

America is at a crossroads, a spiritual turn is desperately needed in this hour of our nation. The days are upon us that God's people can no longer go through the outward religious motions and activities, never truly repenting and turning from their sinful ways and habits. We must stand and be counted, prepared for the battle waged against us a church and the enemies of our nation. God is judging the world and America. It is evident that God is no longer winking at America's national rebellion and open sin. While He is judging the world, He will purge His church, for those will humbly turn and seek Him, while He may be found (Isaiah 55:6).

Repentance will bring a time of refreshing, and restoration; restoration will bring the needed readiness to be the instruments of righteousness 'for such a time as this' (Esther 4:14).

While God's love is unconditional, His promises are conditional, dependent upon our willingness and sincerity of heart to repent and turn from our wicked ways. Sin brings with it its own devastation and consequences in our lives and within a nation. It brings degrees of distress and finally destruction. Scripture tells us sin is a disgrace to any nation (Proverbs 14:34).

Repentance is making an absolute change or turn-around from those things in our lives that have broken our relationship with a loving Creator, things that have severed His blessings, protection and prosperity God desires to release in our lives and once again in our nation.

"Behold, the Lord's hand is not shortened, That it cannot save; Nor His ear heavy, That it cannot hear. But your iniquities have separated you from your God; And your sins have hidden His face from you, So that He will not hear." (Isaiah 59:1, 2). It's not that God can't answer prayers, He can't hear those prayers because of our iniquities.

Nevertheless, for those who are broken and of a contrite heart, God offers forgiveness and restoration. "For thus says the High and Lofty One who inhabits eternity, whose name is Holy: "I dwell in the high and holy place with him who has a contrite and humble spirit, To revive the heart of the contrite ones" (Isaiah 57:15).

Leviticus 26:40-43, explains that God graciously forgave ancient Israel and He will do the same for all who come in the spirit of humility and repentance as shown in 2 Chronicles 7:14. "If My people who are called by name will *humble* themselves, and *pray* and seek My face, and turn from their *wicked ways*, then I will *hear* from heaven, and will *forgive* their sin, and *heal* their land" but let's not forget about vs. 15 "Now My eyes will be *open* and My ears *attentive* to prayer made in this place."

God's people must come to a place of humility, the first step of 2 Chronicles 7:14. Without that first step we will never proceed with the promise(s) attached to what God's Word tells us for the healing and forgiveness He has promised for our individual and corporate lives. With pride of heart we can never meet the requirements of 2 Chronicles 7:14.

It is not that God cannot answer prayers; it is that He cannot hear a prayer from a proud and rebellious heart.

God's requirements are: 1) *humbling* ourselves, 2) prayer, 3) *seeking* His face 4) *turning* from our wicked ways. God then *promises* us He will 1) hear us 2) forgive us and 3) He will heal our land. The Lord concludes by telling us His eyes will be open and His ears *attentive* to our cries. The end results are *forgiveness*, *healing* and *restoration*. Above all, we have positioned ourselves to be embraced by His love and favor upon our lives and nation. The great promise of 2 Chronicles 7:14 is that *if* we do the things God has required, God has obligated Himself to hear our prayers and heal our land.

If God's people, (*conditional*), will meet the requirements of 2 Chronicles 7:14, by the numerous Spirit- filled Christians in the land, and those desiring to see true change that only God can bring, God's hand can again move within our midst that in turn will move God's heart and hand in the affairs of our nation.

God looks today, as He did throughout history for those that will stand in the gap. A glimpse of God's light and truth can very well convince men of humbling themselves in confession of their sins with fervent prayer as a means of escaping God's wrath and obtaining mercy. If there is a mighty outpouring of prayer, faith and righteousness through repentance, God will no doubt answer the fervent cries and petitions of His people to spare the land.

INTERCESSORY PRAYER

None of us can predict the outcome of the moral crisis America finds herself in. America has survived the Civil War, the Spanish-American War, two World Wars, the Korean War, Vietnam, and the Persian Gulf War Now, the ongoing war against terrorism that we are engaged in and changes in Mideast policies along with a brazen defiance of God; as we look within will America survive the internal cultural war for values along with Islamic firebrands determined to destroy her?

In Abraham's dialogue with the Living God he pleaded with the Lord saying "If there are 45 righteous men, will you spare the city?" And God's answer was a resounding, "Yes." The problem was there were not found ten righteous men for God to spare the city of Sodom. Yet, here in America, there are more Bible believing Christians probably than in any other nation of the world. It is fair to say that American Christianity is not bearing the fruit that God intended it to be. What looms on the horizon, a world in chaos, confusion and calamity on all sides of the globe, God's people need to take the authority that has been given them (Luke 10:19).

Prayer, along with genuine repentance will bring about the needed restoration so the true church can respond to the spiritual wickedness and rebellion found from within and without. It is time for the Church to rend their heart before God. The church can no longer fail to recognize the warnings of the coming judgment. If it will not arise in understanding the times and lead the nation in repentance, America will soon fall under the judgment of God in a far more serious and greater way.

Consider the example of Sodom. Abraham was the first intercessor. He pleaded and petitioned God. Sodom did not have a Bible.

If we humble ourselves, pray and truly turn from our wicked ways and cry out to God, though the warfare intensifies, and no change or answers to prayer appear to be evident, we have the confidence to know God is moving on behalf of those whose hearts are committed to Him. We see this in the experience of Daniel.

"And he said to me, "Do not fear, Daniel, for from the first day that you set your heart to understand, and to humble yourself before your God, your words were heard; and I have come because of your words. But the prince of Persia withstood me twenty-one days; and behold, Michael, one of the chief princes, came to help me, for I had been left alone there with the kings of Persia" (Daniel 10: 11,12).

Daniel prayed to the Lord, and made confession: "we have sinned and committed iniquity, we have done wickedly, and rebelled, even departing from Your precepts and Your judgments." Daniel went on to pray, "Neither have we heeded Your servants the prophets, who spoke in Your name to our kings and our princes *(government)* to our fathers and all the people of the land" Daniel 9:5,6.

Scripture clearly points out and reveals to us that the effectual prayers of a righteous man, "has much power and avails much." In the case of Sodom God finally destroyed it. All God can do with a rebellious nation who continues in its rebellion and defiance of God in all aspects of their society is to finally destroy it.

We must pay close attention to what the book of Matthew reveals. It condemns the gospel generation (Matthew 12:41).

When we look at the men of Nineveh, the enemies of God's people, it demonstrates clearly to all that God is not a respecter of persons and is merciful, not willing that one should perish. It was seen a wonder of Divine grace in the repentance and restoration of Nineveh. It was the people of Nineveh who followed the example of a pagan King. It is the best biblical example of national repentance described in the Book of Jonah. Repentance became a national act to prevent national ruin. Even the animals were required to wear sackcloth as a sign of national repentance. Yet, 150 years later Nineveh was found wanting once again. God finally destroyed Nineveh. America cannot miss her hour of Divine visitation.

Realizing God's promises, and His righteous indignation and judgment, such praying brings hope for the future (Jeremiah 29:11). We have overcome through Jesus Christ. The battle has been won and the victory is ours. But the battle still goes on. When we overcome in our individual lives, it is not just for our own sake, it is for the sake of our children and their children's future. It is for the sake of future generations who will receive and inherit the promises of God through our faithfulness.

Revival begins with God's people. Through repentance God first refines and purifies His people. When this is done, He fills them with His mighty power. It is God's heart that we (America) turn from our wicked ways to seek and desire Him once again.

It is a time to remove all barriers within the Church. The Holy Spirit desires to move across denominational lines as the Church sets aside petty differences. God can move mighty mountains on behalf of His people if we meet His requirements.

America, and the nations of the world are being shaken. Listen to what the prophet Haggai spoke; "And I will shake all nations, and the desire of all nations shall come: and I will fill this house with glory, saith the Lord of hosts. The silver is mine, and the gold is mine, saith the Lord of hosts. The glory of this latter house shall be greater than the former, saith the Lord of hosts: and in this place will I give peace, saith the Lord of hosts "(Haggai 2:7-9).

In a time of great distress, uncertainty and a changing tide of events men's hearts are failing them for fear of what is coming upon the earth. Politicians do not have the answer. As America continues to disregard and despise God's righteous statutes and laws, His righteous judgment will continue to be seen throughout our land.

As God is shaking and sifting the nations, He is bringing creation to the Desire of all nations. That 'Desire' is Jesus Christ. His glory will be seen and experienced by all those who desire the Lord and turn to Him. They will stand amidst the chaos, confusion and uncertainty of the times in all areas of their lives in these perilous times we face as a people.

The book of Leviticus gives a frightful conclusion, however, to total disregarding and despising God's statues and judgments:

"And after all this, if you do not obey me, then I will punish you seven times more for your sins, I will break the pride of your power" (Leviticus 26:18,19). We see this plainly, as America continues to experience the devastation if its sin and rebellion. God's hand is still outstretched telling us:

"Seek the Lord while He may be found, Call upon Him while He is near. Let the wicked forsake his way, And the unrighteous man his thoughts: Let him return to the Lord, And he will have mercy on him: And to our God, For He will abundantly pardon" (Isaiah 55:6, 7).

ABOUT THE AUTHOR

Bruce W. Assaf is the author of several books. He brings a comprehensive understanding of the times along with speaking both a profound and prophetic message for this hour. With years of missionary experience, he has been used of the Lord, speaking into the lives of political and religious leaders. He has delivered without compromise the gospel message to numerous congregations in America and throughout the world. He has both pastored and served Christian leaders in various parts of the world.

He is a simple,obedient man with a heart for God. God has promoted him to places of great ministry and influence among the least and greatest of society. Heads of state, heads of religion,to the poor and the despicable. He has not remained silent in delivering the Word of God in its fullness "for such a time as this."

"Bruce's message is full of truth and God's power. He gives it boldly and selflessly."

> – Dr. John Andrews, Director/Colorado Christian University, Lakewood, CO. / Former president of the Colorado State Senate

OTHER BOOKS BY BRUCE W. ASSAF

Charting Your Course to Win God's Way

If My People

Beyond the Veil of Radical Islam: The Coming War

Israel: A Cup of Drunkenness to the Nations

To order additional copies of this book and other books or for speaking engagements, Workshops/Seminars please contact by email trumpet414@att.net or please visit:

www.blowthetrumpetintl.com

BLOW THE TRUMPET
INTERNATIONAL

Read-Study:

P. 40 - 9/11 - P. 7

P. 25 - 26

A - must
to Read - P. (87)

+ P. 29 - 38 - 42

A - List:

P. 11 - 19 -

The word:

P. 21 - 3 -

P. 3 - Sept. 11 - goal

P. 7 -